Psychology
AND
Personal
Growth
IN THE
Torah

MOSAICA PRESS

RABBI SHIMON FEDER

Psychology
AND Personal
Growth
IN THE Torah

PRACTICAL LESSONS
FROM THE RISHONIM

Published by Mosaica Press, Inc.
www.mosaicapress.com
info@mosaicapress.com

Dedicated by Rabbi and Mrs. Larry and Elizabeth Feder
in loving memory of their parents

Mr. Louis Feder
Levi Yitzchak ben Eliezer ז״ל

Mrs. Malka Feder
Malka bas Yerachmiel HaCohen ז״ל

and

Rabbi Moshe Schonfeld
Moshe ben Chaim Baruch ז״ל

Mrs. Pessel Schonfeld
Pessel Lifsha bas Yekusiel Yehudah ז״ל

Despite having survived the Holocaust and life in Siberia during the war, Levi and Malka Feder, z"l, were committed to keeping the flame of Judaism alive in our family for generations to come. They were not interested in amassing material wealth and possessions, nor would our father take any job that required him to work on the Sabbath. He never had the privilege to attend a yeshiva, but he made it his life's goal to provide a quality Torah education for his children and to build a family on the pillars of our *mesorah* (tradition). Our parents also encouraged us to attend college and to pursue our professional goals. The Feders met and married in a post-war refugee camp (DP camp), and they both adamantly refused to renounce their faith after the war. Malka was a deeply nurturing and protective mother whose greatest joy was being able to rise from the ashes and raise a Torah observant family.

Rabbi Moshe and his wife, Pessel Schonfeld, z"l, were both Holocaust survivors who hailed from prominent rabbinic families. Our father was a deeply G-d-fearing and selfless rabbi, *shochet*, and *mohel* who went to great lengths for any family in need of a *bris milah*. He often traveled to far-flung cities to perform circumcisions at the proper time for each baby. He married his wife, Pessel, after the war, also in a DP camp. She was a devout Jewish woman who radiated warmth and kindness. In contrast to her gentle nature, she possessed an inner strength that allowed her to act bravely when the situation warranted. Once, while taking fares as a streetcar conductor during the war, someone recognized her as Jewish and threatened to turn her in. She quickly did what was necessary to remove the passenger from the train, thus saving her own life.

As a result of their ironclad commitment to Judaism, both the Feders and the Schonfelds merited all their children and grandchildren continuing the legacy of Torah observance today.

May their memories be a blessing.

שמואל קמנצקי
Rabbi S. Kamenetsky

2018 Upland Way
Philadelphia, PA 19131

Home: 215-473-2798
Study: 215-473-1212

בעז"ה יום לסדר ראה

לכבוד ידידי הרב ר' ראובן שליט"א

נתכבדתי ושמחתי כאשר בא לפנינו לדין תורה שישבו ביחד על הדבר וסכומו להבטיח של אחרים שם ענינים רבים מאד לעייל לבא תחלה של דני וכו'. ויחם מסורים ויעוץ לכ"ע של אחרים ומי מסור לתוך הענין.

דייני אמצעו לכי שבא כך להעיר של את מחויב להרבה לספסלי לוזי וכו'

דורש לכ' ולביתו שלום וכל טוב

[חתימה]

RSA Rabbinical Seminary of America

ישיבת רבנו ישראל מאיר הכהן זצוקיל
בעל ח"חפץ חיים"

76-01 147th St., Flushing NY 11367
718.268.4700 / Fax: 718.268.4684
office@rabbinical.org

Rabbi Dovid Leibowitz זצוקיל
Founding Rosh HaYeshiva 1933-1941

Rabbi A. Henach Leibowitz זצוקיל
Rosh HaYeshiva 1941-2008

Rabbi Dovid Harris שליט"א
Rosh Yeshiva

Rabbi Akiva Grunblatt שליט"א
Rosh Yeshiva

Dr. Ira Kukin ע"ה
Chairman Emeritus

Dr. Allan Jacob
Chairman of the Board

29 Sh'vat 5781
February 11, 2021

We were excited to hear that our dear talmid, Rabbi Shimon Feder Shlita, has decided to publish a Sefer of his original Shmuzim on the Chumash. We have read several of them and were pleased to see that they are true Mussar insights, developed and presented in the same style as we teach here in our Yeshiva. Rabbi Feder learned in our Yeshiva for many years and developed into a true Ben Torah and Yarei Shomayim. Afterwards, he was inspired to reach out to less affiliated Jews and inspire them to see the greatness and beauty of the Torah. He founded a Kiruv center in Boca Raton, FL and Baruch Hashem, through this endeavor has furthered the Yeshiva's mission of bringing Torah to all Jews. This compilation of his many Divrei Torah will allow many more people to benefit from his insights and ideas.

We give him a Bracha that he should continue his Avodas HaKodesh, and inspire many more Jews to return to their roots. He should see success for many years to come.

B'Hatzlacha Rabba,

Rabbi Dovid Harris   Rabbi Akiva Grunblatt

ק"ק
ישיבה שערי תורה

הלל דייווד
1118 East 12th Street
Brooklyn, NY 11230

ב"ה סיון תש"ם

לכבוד הרב הגאון שלום מרדכי גדול בישראל

לאחדשה"ט - קבלתי האגרת דושמאנא שממרחק של כבודו, ולקנו זבה לבזדוד הכתב
אשר שלח נא לנו נהרא השמאות של רבה שהם רב הגאונים ואחל הגאונים
רב רוב המטאה דבר טוב ונחמים, 6 אמא ארק רוא מעם רק קיקל אדם שה
רבל שולם וברכא!

ונבנן שברויה גידענו לחבירית רבוד, אז זות מאמר רבה ושה דיים ואין חרבו
ולום ובני, ملكך שויר ורשולות לא היח לראות ולוה כנפים לבחל ראה!

נאם
החותם לכבד דתוך
ג'ה דייווד

Table of Contents

Sefer Bereishis

BEREISHIS

NOACH

LECH LECHA

VAYEIRA

CHAYEI SARAH

Sefer Shemos

Sefer Vayikra

Sefer Bamidbar

Sefer Devarim

Holidays

Preface

In His infinite kindness, Hashem has given us the ultimate guidebook to get the most out of life. But how does a finite book provide all the answers to deal with every situation in which we find ourselves? The Torah reads like a storybook replete with life lessons, yet this is only the tip of the iceberg. Beneath the surface lies a wellspring of wisdom that when analyzed sheds light on every possible subject imaginable. Whether it be math, science, medicine, or psychology, all knowledge is encoded within and is waiting for the well-versed mind to uncover it.

The Rishonim possessed the keys to unlock the Torah's endless layers. They were spiritual and intellectual giants who grasped the entire Written and Oral Torah at their fingertips. We are gifted with a treasury of their commentaries on the Torah's verses, and their precise questions and answers fit seamlessly with every letter and word of the Torah. Today, if we have a question that seems to contradict *Rashi*, it is our lack of understanding that is clouding the irrefutable truth in his words. In fact, there is an entire book dedicated to eleven commentators trying to understand and explain *Rashi*!

My *rebbi*, Rabbi Henoch Leibowitz, taught us that we can glean new insights into human psychology and personal growth from the brilliant words of our Rishonim. He gave thousands of talks, spanning over seven decades on *Rashi*, *Ramban*, *Sforno*, *Daas Zekeinim*, and various midrashim that helped people in every area of life. He gave us the tools to give a "*shmuz*" (new insight into life) and to use it to help others to connect to Torah. I have been developing *shmuzim* and teaching them to my students for the past seventeen years. Many of them have come back and said that something we learned helped them in business, relationships, or in improving their self-esteem.

Each *shmuz* consists of a lesson on the *parashah* following a structure of five steps. The first two steps are the question-and-answer for what is bothering the commentator on the verse. Step 3 points out that the commentator does not seem to make sense for the following reasons, and step 4 clarifies the doubt with a new insight into *mussar* and psychology that the Rishon is teaching us. The final step is how we can apply that uplifting lesson to our lives.

I soon realized that these *shmuzim* and how to give a *shmuz* should be an integral part of learning in every home. When my son would bring home friends from *beis midrash* for Shabbos, we would split the boys into several teams, and each would be given a Rishon to explore and share what the *shmuz* is from the Rishonim. The short, predictable format and relevant lessons bring especially meaningful and lively discussions to the Shabbos table.

This is a truly unique *sefer* to be cherished in Jewish homes across the spectrum of Yiddishkeit and all over the world. From secular Jews to *frum beis midrash* boys and everyone in between, Jews of all ages and backgrounds can benefit from these powerful life lessons and utilize the tools to give meaningful *shmuzim* of their own.

Acknowledgments

There are so many people who helped make this *sefer* a reality to whom I owe a debt of gratitude.

I am eternally grateful to my parents, Rabbi and Mrs. Larry Feder, for their support and encouragement in this project and in all facets of my life. Similarly, I would like to thank my in-laws, Mr. and Mrs. Harold Mittel, for supporting our decision to move to East Boca Raton over seventeen years ago—what was then the middle of nowhere—to bring Torah to Jews of all kinds. It was a major decision to leave the comforts of Kew Gardens Hills, Queens, and all that we left behind. If not for our incredible parents, we surely would not be *zocheh* to have started the JEC and to bring the light of Torah to so many.

As a young child, I remember my grandfather Rabbi Moshe Schonfeld was rarely seen without a *sefer* in hand. He had a tremendous love of learning, especially *Chumash*, and could finish the rest of a *pasuk* if someone quoted anywhere in *Tanach* for him. He was my first major influence in developing a love for Torah.

Years later, Rabbi Henoch Leibowitz of Yeshivas Chofetz Chaim taught us, his *talmidim*, how to deliver a *shmuz* rooted in the wisdom of the Rishonim. His influence cultivated within me an even deeper connection to *Chumash*, which ultimately inspired my approach to teaching others and the writing of this book. He taught that the words of the

Rishonim are predicated on an encyclopedic knowledge of the entire Torah and a prophetic ability to seamlessly align their words with its every letter. Furthermore, their insights reveal profound truths about human nature and self-improvement. Studying them can be truly lifechanging.

Rabbi Dovid Harris and Rabbi Akiva Grunblatt of Yeshivas Chofetz Chaim have carried on the legacy of our *rebbi* and have been extremely helpful with this *sefer* by reading through several *shmuzim* before going to print. Thank you for everything you do for the yeshiva and Klal Yisrael.

Rabbi Avraham Semmel has been the go-to Mashgiach of this endeavor and the litmus test to ensure the quality of these talks. Rebbi has always been there for me. I often called him for the final ruling if my *chaverim* and I were unsure if a *shmuz* was proven to follow one approach or another before sending it out to our five-thousand-person list or going to print.

This enormous undertaking could not have been possible without two very integral people on the JEC staff: Rabbi Avrohom Richmond and Mrs. Ally Levin. Rabbi Richmond invested endless time and energy helping to provide input, review, and develop the talks before each one was sent to Mrs. Levin for editing.

When the going got tough, we sought the assistance of Rabbi Chaim Goldstein. If there were any doubts on what the Rishonim were saying, Rabbi Goldstein would spend hours researching the various *sefarim* and databases accessible to him. His contribution of the biography section of this *sefer* is a valuable resource that provides informative synopses about the commentators referenced in this book.

When the world hit pause during the onset of the COVID pandemic and I was inspired to send weekly *d'var Torah* emails, which later culminated in this book, Alexandra Cender and Avi Friedman of the JEC staff played an important role in the project. To the rest of the JEC staff: Rabbi Peled, Rabbi Jacob, Mrs. Rikki Stein, Rabbi Moshe Goldstein, and Mrs. Taly Menashehoff, the JEC would not be what it is without your selfless dedication to our students.

My dear *chavrusa* of many years, Rabbi Avraham Sussman, listened patiently to each *shmuz* and offered valuable insights and comments. Without him, this would have never come to fruition. Thank you for your valuable input, especially during the time we were supposed to be learning Gemara every day!

I would like to thank my brother-in-law Rav Noach Light of East Boca Kehilla, for his support on this project, wise counsel, and being *marbitz Torah*. I am truly blessed to be a part of his *shul* and the East Boca community.

There are no words to express the gratitude I have to my wife, Nechama. All my successes are credited to her unwavering encouragement, advice, and allowing me to devote countless hours to this book and the JEC. Without her endless support, I would not be who I am today. Thank you to our children, Moshe, Riva, Malka, Avraham, Adina, and Rusi for always being a part of the *kiruv* and Torah growth happening in our home. May we be *zocheh* to continue, with the help of Hashem, seeing *nachas* from you.

Thank you to all my students, friends, and generous supporters of this project. We could not do it without you.

Lastly, thank you to Rav Yaacov Haber, Rabbi Doron Kornbluth, and the entire Mosaica Press staff for partnering with me and making this vision a reality. It has been a pleasure to work with you. May we all share in the merit of inspiring thousands of *neshamos*!

Sefer Bereishis

BEREISHIS

Jealousy: Taming the Green-Eyed Monster

Dedicated by Chaim and Samantha Hirsch in memory of his father Refael Mordechai ben Yitzchak

בראשית ג:ו: וַתֵּרֶא הָאִשָּׁה כִּי טוֹב הָעֵץ לְמַאֲכָל וְכִי תַאֲוָה הוּא לָעֵינַיִם וְנֶחְמָד הָעֵץ לְהַשְׂכִּיל וַתִּקַּח מִפִּרְיוֹ וַתֹּאכַל וַתִּתֵּן גַּם לְאִישָׁהּ עִמָּהּ וַיֹּאכַל:

רש"י: ותתן גם לאישה. שֶׁלֹּא תָמוּת הִיא וְיִחְיֶה הוּא, וְיִשָּׂא אַחֶרֶת.

Parashas *Bereishis* recounts the episode of Adam and Chavah eating from the Forbidden Fruit in the Garden of Eden and the decree of death.

> And the woman perceived that the tree was good for eating and that it was a delight to the eyes, and that the tree was desirable as a means to wisdom, and she took of its fruit and ate; and she gave also to her husband **with her** and he ate. (Bereishis 3:6)

3

Q on the verse *Rashi* is perplexed. Why does the verse say, "**with her**"? If there's nothing extra in the Torah, why not just say, "and she gave her husband, and he ate"?

A of the commentator He answers that in the moment when Chavah had taken a bite, before Adam had done so, she believed she would die and was concerned that he might live on and marry someone else. In that split-second of jealousy, she gave Adam the fruit so he would accompany her in the decree of death.

Q on the commentator *Rashi* begs the following questions:

1. We know Adam and Chavah were made for one another and loved each other tremendously. Why would she think of doing such a terrible thing to him?
2. What are the chances that, even if Adam lived, he would marry someone else? G-d already made a huge miracle by creating Chavah from Adam's body and maybe He will not do that again.
3. If Chavah died, she would no longer be in this world, so why should she care about what happens to Adam after her passing?

New insight *Rashi* shows just how poisonous jealousy can be, causing a person to behave despicably even toward loved ones. In the case of Chavah, this was true despite her deep love for her husband and the very remote possibility of him remarrying—and this was despite the fact that she would not even be around to see it!

Lesson for life The *Orchos Tzaddikim* brings that there are two types of jealousy. The first is when we desire what our neighbor has and do everything in our power to attain it. This often comes at a steep cost to us and our family. "I don't mind that you have it; I just want it too."

The second, as illustrated here, is far more dangerous. This type of jealousy is only satisfied by bringing another person down to our lower level. For example, if a person has a booming business, the jealous person is only happy once the other person's business is destroyed. Let us be on guard not to poison our minds and hearts with jealousy, while constantly striving to be grateful for all that we have.

Schmoozing Wisely

*Dedicated by Chaim and Samantha Hirsch in memory
of his father Refael Mordechai ben Yitzchak*

בראשית ד:ח: וַיֹּאמֶר קַיִן אֶל הֶבֶל אָחִיו וַיְהִי בִּהְיוֹתָם בַּשָּׂדֶה וַיָּקָם
קַיִן אֶל הֶבֶל אָחִיו וַיַּהַרְגֵהוּ:

בראשית רבה כב:ז: וַיֹּאמֶר קַיִן אֶל הֶבֶל אָחִיו וַיְהִי בִּהְיוֹתָם וגו'
(בראשית ה, ח), עַל מָה הָיוּ מְדַיְּנִים, אָמְרוּ בּוֹאוּ וְנַחֲלֹק אֶת
הָעוֹלָם, אֶחָד נָטַל הַקַּרְקָעוֹת וְאֶחָד נָטַל אֶת הַמִּטַּלְטְלִין, דֵּין אָמַר
אַרְעָא דְּאַתְּ קָאֵם עֲלָהּ דִּידִי, וְדֵין אָמַר מַה דְּאַתְּ לָבֵישׁ דִּידִי, דֵּין
אָמַר חֲלֹץ, וְדֵין אָמַר פְּרַח, מִתּוֹךְ כָּךְ (בראשית ה, ח): וַיָּקָם קַיִן
אֶל הֶבֶל אָחִיו וַיַּהַרְגֵהוּ.

Parashas Bereishis describes the infamous confrontation
between Kayin and Hevel:

Kayin spoke to his brother Hevel. *And it happened
when they were in the field, that Kayin rose up against
his brother Hevel and killed him. (Bereishis 4:8)*

6

The midrash (expounded by *Maharzu* and *Rashi*) tells us that
"Kayin spoke to his brother Hevel" means that Kayin initially
wanted to rile Hevel up in an argument so that he would then
feel more comfortable murdering his brother once things
heated up.

The midrash records the conversation between the brothers.
First, Kayin proposed to divide up the Earth, since they were
the only descendants of Adam and Chavah. Hevel agreed. Then,
Kayin said that because he works the land, he should own all
land, and Hevel, who is a shepherd, should take all movable
items. Kayin continued, "Please get off my land (meaning the
entire planet) together with your sheep," and Hevel retorted,
"I own the sheep and the wool, and you are no longer entitled
to clothing." The quarrel continued to intensify until it became
violent, at which point Kayin jumped Hevel and killed him.

This midrash is difficult to understand. Although Kayin's intention was evil, Hevel had no such motivation. As Hevel began to
realize that this division plan would never work and his brother
was only using it as an excuse to goad him, he should have
walked away. If someone told you the sky was purple, would you
invest time debating him?

This ancient story in the midrash teaches us a relevant and
important insight into human nature. When someone engages
another into a pointless argument or debate, it is so hard for
even the most intelligent and rational person to disengage. This
is why Hevel didn't just walk away.

Hashem elevated us in this world with speech and intellect
far superior to any other creature. Let us be on guard to avoid
getting pulled into worthless and often time-consuming fights.
We should always assess the value of the discussions in which
we partake, ensuring we are making the most of our time and
relationships!

NOACH

Dose of Inspiration

Dedicated by the Zimmerman family:
Risa and Michael, Aaron, Raquel, and Jacqueline.
May the invaluable lessons of this compilation
of parashah insights enlighten the entire world.

בראשית ז:ד: כִּי לְיָמִים עוֹד שִׁבְעָה אָנֹכִי מַמְטִיר עַל הָאָרֶץ
אַרְבָּעִים יוֹם וְאַרְבָּעִים לָיְלָה וּמָחִיתִי אֶת כָּל הַיְקוּם אֲשֶׁר עָשִׂיתִי
מֵעַל פְּנֵי הָאֲדָמָה:

ילקוט שמעוני: דבר אחר ויהי לשבעת הימים מלמד שתלה להן
הקב"ה שבע ימי אבלו של מתושלח הצדיק כדי שיעשו תשובה
ולא עשו.

סנהדרין קח ב: ויהי לשבעת הימים ומי המבול היו על הארץ
(בראשית ז, י) מה טיבם של שבעת הימים? אמר רב אלו ימי
אבילות של מתושלח ללמדך שהספדן של צדיקים מעכבין את
הפורענות לבא.

מהרש"א: גמ' ויהי לשבעת הימים ג' אלו ימי כו'. מיתורא דה'
הידיעה דרשו כן שהן ז' ימים הידועים שהן אבלו של מתושלח
כו' אבל רש"י בחומש הביא דרשה דהכא אקרא דלעיל מיניה

8

דכתיב כי לימים עוד שבעה וגי והוא מבואר דבהספדו של צדיק
אולי יחזרו בתשובה שאין עוד מי שיגן עליהם כי אפס הצדיק.

In *parashas Noach*, before Hashem brings the great flood, He
gives a final warning:

> For **in seven more days' time**, I will send rain upon
> the earth...and I will blot out all existence that I have
> made from upon the face of the ground. (Bereishis 7:4)

Q on the verse Several commentators are bothered: Why would Hashem delay
the rain that will destroy everything on the planet "**in seven
more days' time**"? Noach was instructed to build the Ark for
120 years to warn people that if they did not change their ways,
G-d would destroy the world. Why then the need for an additional seven days?

A of the commentator The *Yalkut Shimoni* and *Talmud Sanhedrin* (108b), as explained by
Maharsha, tell us that Hashem did this because Mesushelach the
righteous had just died, and perhaps people would be inspired
during the *shivah* (seven-day mourning period) to repent from
their evil ways as a result of the realization that Mesushelach's
merit was no longer protecting them, thus leading them to
improve. As a result, Hashem would no longer need to destroy
the world.

Q on the commentator This *Yalkut Shimoni* is troubling! At the time of the flood, the
world had sunk to the deepest levels of sin. Theft was the norm,
and illicit relationships were so widespread that even animals
began to cohabit with other species. The world was so corrupt
that Hashem wanted to destroy everything and start over with
just Noach and his family. Years of warning from Noach that
a flood was imminent fell on deaf ears. So what was the chance
that, given a few more days, people would repent and return to
Hashem? Why did Hashem believe that these seven days could
actually effectuate the meaningful and substantial change that
was needed when 120 years had proven to be ineffective?

New insight

We learn from this *Yalkut Shimoni* an unbelievable lesson! The inspiration during the *shivah* for Mesushelach could ignite emotions, inspiring life changes. Although they were constantly steeped in physical desires and knew it would cost them their lives, that did not stop them from such wicked behavior. However, a shot of inspiration had the potential to propel them to success where they had failed so many times previously, as every *neshamah* is hardwired to recognize the beauty of truth and spirituality.

Lesson for life

Sometimes in life we are at a standstill: We yearn to grow in our prayer, learning, and mitzvos. We often find ourselves stuck in a rut, not enthused to do anything productive. Search for that life-changing dose of inspiration that will make you the best version of yourself.

The Awesome
Responsibility
of Sensitivity

בראשית ז:ז: וַיָּבֹא נֹחַ וּבָנָיו וְאִשְׁתּוֹ וּנְשֵׁי בָנָיו אִתּוֹ אֶל הַתֵּבָה מִפְּנֵי
מֵי הַמַּבּוּל:

רש״י: נח ובניו. הָאֲנָשִׁים לְבַד וְהַנָּשִׁים לְבַד, לְפִי שֶׁנֶּאֶסְרוּ בְּתַשְׁמִישׁ
הַמִּטָּה מִפְּנֵי שֶׁהָעוֹלָם שָׁרוּי בְּצַעַר.

P*arashas Noach* finds Noach and his family preparing to enter the Ark before the great flood destroys the world.

> *Noach, with his sons, his wife, and his sons' wives with*
> *him, went into the Ark because of the waters of the*
> *Flood. (Bereishis 7:7)*

Q on the verse *Rashi* is bothered by the strange grouping in the verse. Isn't it logical to write that they entered the Ark together with their spouses? Why does the verse list the men entering as one, followed by the women?

A of the commentator He answers that this structure hints to G-d's prohibition of marital intimacy while aboard the Ark, because the world was in pain and suffering.

Q on the commentator This *Rashi* is perplexing!

1. Just because the world was suffering, could they not act normally? Furthermore, the world is about to be destroyed, isn't it a mitzvah to begin to repopulate it?
2. The world was inhabited by such evil people that the only solution was to annihilate them. So why should Noach and his family be sensitive to their suffering?
3. Hashem had instructed Noach to build the Ark for 120 years in order to give people ample time to repent, yet they were unfazed. Why should those aboard the Ark feel bad for them?
4. The people had threatened to kill Noach and his family if there should ever be a flood, so G-d stationed lions outside the Ark to protect Noach and his family as they entered. These are people they should care about?

New insight *Rashi* is teaching an important lesson in human sensitivity. Although the world was extremely corrupt and deserved to be destroyed, those aboard the Ark needed to be sympathetic to the fact that humankind would suffer. Therefore, they were instructed to refrain from normal relations during the flood.

Lesson for life There once was a great rabbi during World War II who would sleep only on the floor. Since there was a bed available, his students asked why he did not make use of it. He answered that because so many were being tortured and murdered in Europe, he did not feel comfortable getting a good night's sleep in his own bed. While a vast majority of us do not feel compassion and sensitivity on his level, there is so much that we can do. Let us make sensitivity toward others a priority and genuinely feel for others.

LECH LECHA

Defining Moments

בראשית יג:יא: וַיִּבְחַר לוֹ לוֹט אֵת כָּל כִּכַּר הַיַּרְדֵּן וַיִּסַּע לוֹט מִקֶּדֶם וַיִּפָּרְדוּ אִישׁ מֵעַל אָחִיו:

חזקוני: ויפרדו איש מעל אחיו פרידה גדולה היתה, וכן הוא אומר לא יבוא עמוני ומואבי וגו' (דברים כג:ד)

In *Parashas Lech Lecha*, Avraham's nephew Lot decides to leave his uncle's household and settle in Sodom and Gomorrah, the most corrupt and immoral cities of that time.

> So Lot chose for himself the whole plain of the Jordan...thus **they parted, one from his brother**. (Bereishis 13:11)

Q on the verse The *Chizkuni* is bothered by a question. What extra information do the words, "**they parted, one from his brother**," give us? If Lot chose to move away, isn't it obvious that he separated from his uncle?

A of the commentator He answers that the Torah highlights this because it is a defining moment for Lot and his future descendants for all time. The decision to split from his righteous family and move to Sodom and Gomorrah was the beginning of Lot's tragic downfall. It marked the start of Lot's descent into such depravity that his descendants—the Ammonites and Moabites—would never be able to marry into the Jewish People.

Q on the commentator This *Chizkuni* is difficult to understand. Why is moving away from his uncle's influence such a crime, warranting that his descendants could no longer marry into the Jewish nation? All Lot did was make a poor decision with regard to relocating his family. He had not committed any actual sins, such as thievery, cruelty, or lewd acts for which the people of Sodom and Gomorrah were infamous!

New insight We learn from this *Chizkuni* an important life lesson. Although it appears that Lot only made one misstep, this was actually the catalyst that propelled him toward sin for the rest of his life. Therefore, the Torah emphasized, "they parted, one from his brother," because this moment initiated a life contrary to the Torah values that Lot had been constantly learning from his uncle, Avraham.

Lesson for life In life, we often face crucial decisions such as where to live, whom to associate with, and the type of lifestyle we want to live. These seemingly small moments can have lifelong ramifications for the best, or G-d forbid, for the worst. We must pay careful attention to ensure that our choices line up with a life of true goodness and spirituality.

Blinded by Ego

לעילוי נשמת בערל בן עבר הלוי

*A man who with tremendous מסירת נפש and courage
embarked upon a personal לך לך journey with his family,
and as a result was זוכה to see grandchildren and great
grandchildren living a life of תורה ומצות*

בראשית יג:יד–טו: וַה׳ אָמַר אֶל אַבְרָם אַחֲרֵי הִפָּרֶד לוֹט מֵעִמּוֹ
שָׂא נָא עֵינֶיךָ וּרְאֵה מִן הַמָּקוֹם אֲשֶׁר אַתָּה שָׁם צָפֹנָה וָנֶגְבָּה וָקֵדְמָה
וָיָמָּה: כִּי אֶת כָּל הָאָרֶץ אֲשֶׁר אַתָּה רֹאֶה לְךָ אֶתְּנֶנָּה וּלְזַרְעֲךָ עַד
עוֹלָם:

ספורנו: אחרי הפרד לוט ולא אמר זה בהיות לוט עמו פן בכבודו
יתימרו ויתגאו לוט ורועיו ויתאמצו לגזול.

Parashas Lech Lecha relates a quarrel between Avraham and
his nephew Lot. Lot's herdsmen allowed their sheep to
graze from other people's land, causing Avraham's shepherds to
admonish this behavior as stealing. Avraham now asks Lot to
move to a nearby land with his livestock.

*G-d said to Avraham **after Lot had parted from him**,*
"Raise your eyes and look out from the land where you
are: northward, southward, eastward, and westward.
For all the land that you see, to you will I give it, and to
your descendants forever." (Bereishis 13:14–15)

Q on the verse The *Sforno* wonders why the Torah specifies that G-d spoke to Avraham "**after Lot had parted from him.**" Didn't G-d appear to Avraham all the time?

A of the commentator He answers that while G-d appeared to Avraham often, He held off visiting during this quarrel. Had G-d appeared while Lot was present, he and his shepherds would have haughtily believed that G-d was honoring them, which would have emboldened them to steal more. Therefore, at this juncture, G-d only revealed Himself to Avraham "after Lot had parted from him."

Q on the commentator This *Sforno* is hard to understand. If G-d would have come to visit now but had only spoken to Avraham, what honor and respect would He be showing to Lot? None! Furthermore, the whole reason behind the separation behind Avraham and Lot was because of Lot's stealing!

New insight We see from this *Sforno* that although, objectively, G-d was not honoring Lot and his shepherds nor condoning their corrupt behavior, Lot and his crew would distort the visit and twist it to fit their egotistical narrative. They would convince themselves that G-d was there in their honor, which would encourage them to continue on their evil path!

Lesson for life We all go through life seeing things through different lenses. However, our egos color those lenses to show a whole new reality. G-d Himself can come to visit someone and another person will convince himself that G-d came in his honor. Let us strive to act with humility, and let us merit to see the world with clarity.

VAYEIRA

Social Responsibility

Dedicated by Moshe, Riva, Malka, Avraham,
Adina, and Rusi Feder in honor of their parents,
Rabbi Shimon and Nechama Feder

בראשית יט:ד–ה: טֶרֶם יִשְׁכָּבוּ וְאַנְשֵׁי הָעִיר אַנְשֵׁי סְדֹם נָסַבּוּ עַל
הַבַּיִת מִנַּעַר וְעַד זָקֵן כָּל הָעָם מִקָּצֶה: וַיִּקְרְאוּ אֶל לוֹט וַיֹּאמְרוּ לוֹ
אַיֵּה הָאֲנָשִׁים אֲשֶׁר בָּאוּ אֵלֶיךָ הַלָּיְלָה הוֹצִיאֵם אֵלֵינוּ וְנֵדְעָה אֹתָם:

רש"י: כל העם מקצה. מִקְצֵה הָעִיר עַד הַקָּצֶה, שֶׁאֵין אֶחָד מֵהֶם
מוֹחֶה בְּיָדָם, שֶׁאֲפִלוּ צַדִּיק אֶחָד אֵין בָּהֶם.

שפתי חכמים: שאין אחד מוחה בידם כו'. רצונו לומר וכי אפשר
דבר זה שמקום קטן כזה דהיינו מה שסובב הבית יחזיק כל אנשי
עיר ומתרץ שאין אחד מהם מוחה בידם וכיון שלא מיחו הרי הן
כאילו עצמן עשו.

In *Parashas Vayeira*, the Torah describes Lot's hospitality and
the response of the people of Sodom.

They had not yet lain down when the townspeople,
Sodomites, converged upon the house, from young to

old, **all the people** *from every quarter. And they had
called to Lot and said to him, "Where are the men who
came to you tonight? Bring them out to us that we may
do cruel things to them." (Bereishis 19:4–5)*

Q on the verse *Rashi* is bothered by a question. How is it possible for "**all the people**" of the town to surround a single home?

A of the commentator *Rashi* (as expounded by *Sifsei Chachamim*) answers that, of course, they could not fit **all the people** of the town around the home, but since no one stood up to protest this exceedingly evil behavior, it was as if everyone had participated in the terrible revolt against Lot's guests.

Q on the commentator This *Rashi* is mind-boggling! The cruelty that the locals wanted to perpetrate was extreme (see commentaries). But why would those who stayed home because they were scared to stand up against the masses or felt that their efforts would be in vain be culpable for the attack as well? They did nothing wrong.

New insight We learn from this *Rashi* that if one witnesses cruelty or injustice and does nothing to stop it, he is responsible—on some level—as if he had a part in it! This is true even when he had nothing to do with the issue at hand and felt that his attempts to help would be futile. We have a social responsibility to speak up and get involved, even if there is a possibility of being harmed.

Lesson for life At times, we feel strongly about an issue, yet we do not get involved for various reasons. We may feel threatened or insecure about successfully effectuating change. The Torah is teaching us that we have a moral obligation to try to make a difference. By not doing so, we are contributing, on some level, to the issue at hand. Whether our efforts are big or small, we are obligated to do something. As the dictum goes, "You do your best, and G-d will do the rest!"

The Importance
of Checking In

*Dedicated by Moshe, Riva, Malka, Avraham,
Adina, and Rusi Feder in honor of their parents
Rabbi Shimon and Nechama Feder*

בראשית כב:א: וַיְהִי אַחַר הַדְּבָרִים הָאֵלֶּה וְהָאֱלֹקִים נִסָּה אֶת
אַבְרָהָם וַיֹּאמֶר אֵלָיו אַבְרָהָם וַיֹּאמֶר הִנֵּנִי:

רשב"ם: ויהי אחר הדברים האלה—אחר הדברים שכרת אברהם
ברית לאבימלך לו ולנינו ולנכדו של אברהם ונתן לו שבע כבשות
הצאן וחרה אפו של הקב"ה על זאת, שהרי ארץ פלשתים ניתן
לאברהם...נתגאיתה בבן שנתתי לך לכרות ברית ביניכם ובין
בניהם. ועתה לך והעלהו לעולה וראה מה הועילה כריתות
ברית שלך.

In *Parashas Vayeira*, Avraham is challenged and grows closer
to Hashem as he passes ten very difficult tests. The final test
was the "Binding of Yitzchak."

And *it happened after these things that G-d tested*
Avraham…(Bereishis 22:1)

Q on the verse

The *Rashbam* is bothered by a question. The wording, "**it**
happened after these things that G-d tested Avraham,"
connotes a wrongdoing by Avraham that caused this final test.
What was it?

A of the commentator

The *Rashbam* uses a novel approach to answer this: Avraham
was overjoyed by the birth of a son after so many years of being
childless. This caused him to feel slightly haughty and mistakenly sign an unwarranted peace treaty with Avimelech. This
warranted a punishment from G-d, who tested Avraham in an
exceedingly difficult manner with the "Binding of Yitzchak."

Q on the commentator

The million-dollar question is why he proceeded to act on this
idea without first checking in with G-d. G-d told Avraham that
he would one day inherit this land, and Avraham had an idea.
Perhaps a good idea, perhaps not, but why not ask G-d when he
spoke to Him next? It would have been a pretty simple thing for
him to do, as he spoke to G-d regularly.

New insight

The *Rashbam* is teaching us an invaluable life lesson. When we
think we know the answer, we rarely check in with those who
are greater or more experienced than we are. We simply go for
it! That is why Avraham had a misstep here and was punished.

Lesson for life

Too often, we get into an argument with someone else only to
be asked by our opposition, "Why don't we ask someone else
whom we both trust, who is right?" And the response is, "I don't
need to ask anyone; of course I'm right!" We need to realize that
our judgment is often clouded by "blind spots" that can lead us
down a path of major failures. Conversely, major accomplishments and success await us if we can only be humble enough to
listen to others.

The Transformative Power of Torah

Dedicated by Barak Baver in memory of his father
Nechemia Aryeh Leib Peretz ben Eliyahu HaLevi

בראשית כג:ו: שְׁמָעֵנוּ אֲדֹנִי נְשִׂיא אֱלֹקִים אַתָּה בְּתוֹכֵנוּ בְּמִבְחַר קְבָרֵינוּ קְבֹר אֶת מֵתֶךָ אִישׁ מִמֶּנּוּ אֶת קִבְרוֹ לֹא יִכְלֶה מִמְּךָ מִקְּבֹר מֵתֶךָ:

חזקוני ויקרא יח:ג: כמעשה ארץ מצרים, וכמעשה ארץ כנען ר' יוסי הגלילי אומר אחר ששקל מעשה ארץ מצרים כמעשה ארץ כנען ומעשה ארץ כנען כמעשה ארץ מצרים למה זכו הכנענים לשבת בארצם ארבעים ושבע שנים שנאמר וחברון שבע שנים נבנתה לפני צוען מצרים אלא בשכר שקברו את אברהם אבינו במערת המכפלה זכו (תורת כהנים פרשא ח, ו).

תורת כהנים אחרי מות פרשה ח:ו: מפני מה זכו הכנענים לישב בארצם ארבעים ושבע שנים...אלא בשביל שכר שכבדו את אברהם אבינו שאמרו לו (בראשית כג ו) שמענו אדוני נשיא אלקים אתה בתוכינו, בני אדם שכבדו את אברהם אבינו זכו לישב בארצם שבע וארבעים שנה.

22

I n *Parashas Chayei Sarah*, Avraham approaches the Canaanites seeking a burial plot for his wife, Sarah. The Canaanites respond:

> "Hear us, my lord: You are a prince of G-d in our midst;
> in the choicest of our burial places bury your dead..."
> (Bereishis 23:6)

The commentator explains

The *Chizkuni* (Leviticus 18:3) and *Toras Kohanim* (8:6) explain that the Canaanites merited to keep the Land of Israel for an additional forty-seven years because they treated Avraham with the utmost respect here.

Q on the commentator

This begs the question. The Canaanites were undeserving of this. They were among the most corrupt nations of the world during that time, and the Torah teaches that the Holy Land expels such people. Furthermore, what is the big deal that they were impressed by the holy Avraham and treated him nicely? Does this small mitzvah of *kavod* (giving honor) really justify allowing a nation of millions to inhabit a land for decades?

New insight

The *Chizkuni* teaches us an incredible lesson. Showing honor to one who has saturated himself with Torah is of major importance, not just a small nicety, so much so that this one conversation that took place 363 years before the Jews inhabited the Land warranted the Canaanites to spend forty-seven extra years there. So great is the merit of this mitzvah!

Lesson for life

Honoring the Torah and those who learn it is of vital importance, especially if we appreciate how much Torah study can transform us as human beings. Just recently, the Jewish world mourned the passing of two giants among men: Rabbi Dovid Feinstein and Rabbi Jonathan Sacks. In addition to inspiring thousands with their exceptional wisdom and insight, they possessed the rare ability to make everyone who came into contact with them feel special.

What was the secret of their success? Did their parents or teachers teach them better manners? The answer is that they spent a tremendous amount of time immersing themselves in the Torah and its values. That is how they became greater and greater. Let us be inspired by their amazing stories and commit to becoming more learned in our Torah study to reach new heights in our interpersonal relationships.

Bribery Blinds

Dedicated by Barak Baver in memory of Hinda Bas Meir

בראשית כד:א–ד: וְאַבְרָהָם זָקֵן בָּא בַּיָּמִים וַה' בֵּרַךְ אֶת אַבְרָהָם
בַּכֹּל: וַיֹּאמֶר אַבְרָהָם אֶל עַבְדּוֹ זְקַן בֵּיתוֹ הַמֹּשֵׁל בְּכָל אֲשֶׁר לוֹ שִׂים
נָא יָדְךָ תַּחַת יְרֵכִי: וְאַשְׁבִּיעֲךָ בַּה' אֱלֹקֵי הַשָּׁמַיִם וֵאלֹקֵי הָאָרֶץ
אֲשֶׁר לֹא תִקַּח אִשָּׁה לִבְנִי מִבְּנוֹת הַכְּנַעֲנִי אֲשֶׁר אָנֹכִי יוֹשֵׁב בְּקִרְבּוֹ:
כִּי אֶל אַרְצִי וְאֶל מוֹלַדְתִּי תֵּלֵךְ וְלָקַחְתָּ אִשָּׁה לִבְנִי לְיִצְחָק:

ספורנו: ואברהם זקן. ומפני עשרו דאג שמא איזה אדם בלתי הגון
ירבה שוחד לעבדו כדי שיבחר בבתו ולא ישתדל להשיג אשה
הגונה לבנו. ולכן הוצרך להשביע את עבדו על כל אלה

In *Parashas Chayei Sarah*, Avraham tasks his servant, Eliezer, with finding a match for his son, Yitzchak.

Now Avraham was old, well on in years, and Hashem had blessed Avraham with everything. And Avraham said to his servant, the elder of his household who controls all that is his: "Place now your hand under my thigh. And I will have you swear by Hashem, God of heaven and God of earth, that you not take a wife for

25

*my son from the daughters of the Canaanites, among
whom I dwell. Rather, to my land and to my kindred
shall you go and take a wife for my son, for Yitzchak."
(Bereishis 24:1–4)*

The *Sforno* wants to know: Why did Avraham require his trusted
servant Eliezer to take an oath?

He answers that as Avraham was getting older, he had several
concerns regarding finding a match for Yitzchak, the progenitor
of the Jewish nation. He feared that his great wealth might cause
someone to bribe his right-hand man, Eliezer, into arranging
a *shidduch* that was not totally up to Avraham's standards.

This *Sforno* is puzzling. Many commentaries expound the vir-
tues of Eliezer, the trusted servant of Avraham. He was wise in
Torah knowledge, kept the mitzvos, and was trusted in all of
Avraham's estate. Eliezer joined a civil war to fight alongside
Avraham at great peril to his life. How can Avraham even sug-
gest that Eliezer would be susceptible to a bribe?

Sforno is teaching that when money is on the line, even some
of the most scrupulous people can be affected. Even the great
Eliezer can be bribed to accept a candidate who may check most
of the boxes, but not all, if money is at stake. And so, Avraham,
knowing human nature, protected Eliezer from this potential
mistake by having him swear.

How careful we must be to check that all our actions are done
with the right reasons and motivations behind them. People
may physically bribe us or even complement or flatter us in such
a way that we want to go above and beyond the norm for them.
We must always be on guard to follow our moral compass and
avoid bribery that can lead us down the wrong path.

TOLDOS

The Power of Empathy

---

*Dedicated by Avi and Tali Friedman in honor
of their parents Mr. and Mrs. Matti Friedman
and Dr. and Mrs. Salomon Imiak*

בראשית כה:כב: וַיִּתְרֹצְצוּ הַבָּנִים בְּקִרְבָּהּ וַתֹּאמֶר אִם כֵּן לָמָּה זֶּה
אָנֹכִי וַתֵּלֶךְ לִדְרֹשׁ אֶת ה':

רש"י: ויתרוצצו. עַ"כ הַמִּקְרָא הַזֶּה אוֹמֵר דָּרְשֵׁנִי, שֶׁסָּתַם מַה הִיא
רְצִיצָה זוֹ.

שפתי חכמים: ר"ל כיון שסתם מה היא רציצה זו א"כ מסתמא
היא רציצה כדרך שאר נשים מעוברות וא"כ למה כתיב אח"כ
א"כ למה זה אנכי וכי אינה יודעת שיהי' לה צער העיבור אלא
ודאי כמו שדרש רז"ל שהוא לשון ריצה דאין דרך להיות כן
בשאר נשים וע"ז פירש"י אח"כ ותאמר א"כ צער העיבור שלי
יותר משאר נשים א"כ למה זה אנכי.

מזרחי: שכשאמרה להן הגיע לכן צער כזה אמרו לה לא ואז
אמרה היא א"כ הוא צער העבור שלי שלא כמנהג הלואי לא
עברתי דאל"כ מאי אם כן הוא צער העבור הלואי לא עברתי
דקאמרה נוהג כל המעוברות כן הוא ועוד ממה שהיתה מחזרת
על פתחיהן ושואלת אם אירע להן ככה נראה שאם היו אומרות

27

לה מנהג כל המעוברות כן הוא שוב לא היתה חוששת מהצער
ואם כן אם אמרו לה שדרך העבור כן הוא למה חזרה ואמרה אם
כן הוא צער העבור הלואי לא עברתי.

I n *Parashas Toldos*, the Torah relates how Rivkah was feeling
as she was expecting for the first time:

> **The children agitated within her,** and she said, "**If so,
> why am I thus**?" And she went to inquire of Hashem.
> (Bereishis 25:22)

The
commentator
explains

Rashi (expounded by *Sifsei Chachamim*) explains that "**the
children agitated within her**" describes Rivkah's intense pain
during pregnancy. This leads her to regret wanting to bear children, as she declares, "**If so, why am I thus**?" as the pain was far
more intense than she had ever anticipated. *Sifsei Chachamim*
further explains that Rivkah's pain was worse than **all the rest
of the women**, and because of this, she was in complete despair.

Q on the
commentator

What does the comparison to "**all the rest of the women**"
have to do with anything? Rivkah, of course, read the book
What to Expect When You're Expecting, and she knew there
would be a level of discomfort and suffering while pregnant.
Furthermore, she knew prophetically that she would be the
matriarch of the Jewish nation and prayed fervently for two
decades for children. Why did knowing that her pain was worse
than anyone else's bring her such hopelessness? Shouldn't she
be able to bear any amount of hardship to be the mother of the
Jewish People?

New
insight

Rashi with *Sifsei Chachamim* (and *Mizrachi*) are teaching us an
incredible lesson. Even though Rivkah knew intellectually how
important her role as matriarch of the Jewish People was and
how elated she should be, emotionally she was not able to cope
because there was no one there who could understand her degree of suffering. Had someone else come along who had been
through the exact same experience, this solidarity and empathy

would have given her the strength and impetus to carry her though this difficult time.

Lesson for life One may think that there is a limit to the amount a person can handle, but nothing could be further from the truth! When we are going through a hardship, we may be overwhelmed and feel that we cannot handle the situation. We may turn to friends, leaders, or doctors to help us get through it. There is someone even more supportive, however, who can help us tap into our inner reservoirs of strength: a person who has been in our shoes. When enduring a hardship that seems to be impossible, connecting with someone who has overcome the same battle can give us the encouragement we need to succeed. On the flipside, we may possess life experiences that can be an amazing source of strength to others. May we use our life experiences to support others, and may we find strength and inspiration in others who have endured our challenges.

A Face Only
a Mother Could Love

*Dedicated by Avi and Tali Friedman in honor
of their children Naomi, Elisheva, and Hillel.
May they continue to be a source of Nachas to us
and all who come in contact with them.*

בראשית כח:ה: וַיִּשְׁלַח יִצְחָק אֶת יַעֲקֹב וַיֵּלֶךְ פַּדֶּנָה אֲרָם אֶל לָבָן
בֶּן בְּתוּאֵל הָאֲרַמִּי אֲחִי רִבְקָה אֵם יַעֲקֹב וְעֵשָׂו:

חזקוני: אם יעקב ועשו. שלטובת שניהם נתכוונה כדכתיב למה
אשכל גם שניכם יום אחד.

At the end of *Parashas Toldos*, Yaakov's parents instruct
him to go to Uncle Lavan's home to find a wife.

*So Yitzchak sent away Yaakov, and he went toward
Paddan-Aram, to Lavan the son of Besuel the
Aramean, brother of Rivkah, **mother of Yaakov and
Esav**. (Bereishis 28:5)*

30

Q on the verse *Chizkuni* has a question on this verse. The Torah had previously recorded Rivkah's birth of these boys. So why reiterate that Rivkah is the "**mother of Yaakov and Esav**"?

A of the commentator He answers that these words highlight just how deeply Rivkah loved both of her twin sons.

Q on the commentator This *Chizkuni* is confusing. On the one hand, everyone knows how intensely a mother loves her children. However, Esav did not succeed in fooling his mother like he did his father. She knew that he was conniving and pure evil. She was aware that he threatened the life of his brother, Yaakov, and that this hunter and murderer was serious. How then can we talk about the intense motherly love she had for both of them in the same sentence?

New insight We learn from this *Chizkuni* an insight into a mother's love for her child. Unlike a mother whose blind love for her son may cause her to insist on his innocence even as he walks down Death Row, Rivkah knew the score. Despite Esav's failings, his mother, Rivkah, had a profound feeling of love for him because he was her child. She loved both of her children, the good one and the evil one, and she never gave up that feeling or the title of being their mother.

Lesson for life No matter what, our parents and our Father in Heaven have a deep and intense love for us. Whether our parents show it properly or not, or give encouragement or not, ingrained in their essence is that feeling of love. At each turn, they are there for us and rooting for us. Let this love give us encouragement in everything we do.

Labels Belong on Cans

Dedicated by Robyn and Alan Rice
in memory of Alan's parents,
Riva Esse bas Elchonon Dov, Avraham ben Yitzchak

בראשית כט:יח: וַיֶּאֱהַב יַעֲקֹב אֶת רָחֵל וַיֹּאמֶר אֶעֱבָדְךָ שֶׁבַע שָׁנִים
בְּרָחֵל בִּתְּךָ הַקְּטַנָּה:

חזקוני: שאינה חשובה בעיניך כלאה הגדולה כי רועה היא ועל כן
אמר להיות רועה תחתיה.

In *Parashas Vayeitzei*, Yaakov is very taken by Rachel, so he makes the following offer to his Uncle Lavan.

> *Yaakov loved Rachel, so he said, "I will work for you seven years, for Rachel, **your younger daughter**."* (Bereishis 29:18)

 The *Chizkuni* is bothered by why Yaakov referred to Rachel in the verse as the "**younger daughter**"? Doesn't everyone know Rachel is the younger daughter?

A of the commentator

He answers that Yaakov was in essence telling Lavan, "Although you do not accord the same respect to Rachel as you do her older sister, Leah, because Rachel is a lowly shepherdess, I value her greatly and would like to have her hand in marriage."

Q on the commentator

This *Chizkuni* is puzzling. Who said that Uncle Lavan did not respect or value Rachel? Furthermore, he is the one who gave his daughter this job in the first place. Why doesn't he call Yaakov presumptive and throw him out?

New insight

We learn from this *Chizkuni* an unbelievable lesson. In Yaakov's greatness and supreme ability to pick up on nuances, he sensed a negative vibe from Lavan towards his daughter. Lavan looked down upon Rachel as being a lowly shepherdess, even though he was the one who gave her the job. Therefore, she was viewed as small in his eyes.

Lesson for life

We often accord importance to others based on their occupation. Someone who holds a job title like doctor or CEO is viewed as special and deserving of utmost respect. A grocery bagger at the local store, on the other hand, is often rated as second-class. May we always view everyone as special, unique, and prominent because they were created in the image of Hashem!

Gratitude Brings Happiness

Dedicated by Robyn and Alan Rice in memory
of Robyn's Parents, Michael ben Yaakov, Osnot bas Yosef

בראשית ל:כ–כא: וַתֹּאמֶר לֵאָה זְבָדַנִי אֱלֹקִים אֹתִי זֵבֶד טוֹב
הַפַּעַם יִזְבְּלֵנִי אִישִׁי כִּי יָלַדְתִּי לוֹ שִׁשָּׁה בָנִים וַתִּקְרָא אֶת שְׁמוֹ זְבֻלוּן:
וְאַחַר יָלְדָה בַּת וַתִּקְרָא אֶת שְׁמָהּ דִּינָה:

רבנו בחיי: וזהו שאמרו רז"ל חכמי האמת לאה התפללה וחזרה
נקבה, וכוונתם בזה לומר כי היתה לאה ראויה להנתן לה יוסף
אלא שלא רצתה וחזרה נקבה, כי לא חששה לכל מה שלמטה
מזבולן וע"כ באה לידי מכשול ואירע בה מה שאירע.

Parashas *Vayeitzei* recalls the story of Leah's seventh
pregnancy.

*"For I have born six sons."...Afterwards, she bore
a daughter and she called her name Dinah. (Bereishis
30:20–21)*

Rabbeinu Bachaya tells us that the child in Leah's womb was supposed to be Yosef. Having already been blessed with six sons who each represented one of the twelve tribes, she was less concerned with this pregnancy. She did not fully appreciate the opportunity to carry another founding figure of the Jewish People, and because of this, Hashem miraculously switched the baby in her womb to Dinah.

This fascinating insight from Rabbeinu Bachaya is puzzling. What caused the matriarch Leah to not fully appreciate this? She was extremely righteous, bright, and a prophetess who knew that the Jewish nation would be built from her children. How did she not treasure this monumental opportunity to birth the one who would become known as "Yosef the Righteous"?

Rabbeinu Bachaya is teaching us an insight into human nature. Although Leah was appreciative that she was expecting for a seventh time, she lost sight of what was at hand. On some slight level, she was not as excited as she had been for the previous births and was more *laissez-faire*. And because of this, she lost the tremendous opportunity to have Yosef, who would become the most important of the brothers on many levels.

In life, it is very difficult to always be excited, happy, and grateful for all the good things that come our way. When it is the first child, business deal, or home purchase, we are over the moon with happiness. As time goes on or as we accumulate more, we become used to our blessings, and they no longer exhilarate us. Our job is to learn to always view all goodness with a freshness as if we are receiving it for the very first time. And with that, we will always be happy!

VAYISHLACH

How to Win Friends and Influence People

Dedicated by Mr. and Mrs. Harold and Judith Mittel
in memory of their parents,
Mr. and Mrs. Abe and Rita Rice

בראשית לב:ה–ו: וַיְצַו אֹתָם לֵאמֹר כֹּה תֹאמְרוּן לַאדֹנִי לְעֵשָׂו כֹּה אָמַר עַבְדְּךָ יַעֲקֹב עִם לָבָן גַּרְתִּי וָאֵחַר עַד עָתָּה: וַיְהִי לִי שׁוֹר וַחֲמוֹר צֹאן וְעֶבֶד וְשִׁפְחָה וָאֶשְׁלְחָה לְהַגִּיד לַאדֹנִי לִמְצֹא חֵן בְּעֵינֶיךָ:

רלב״ג: התועלת הראשון הוא במדות. והוא שראוי למי שיש לו שונא וירצה שתסור שנאתו ממנו שתקרב אליו בכל עוז ויגיד לו עניניו כי בזה מהתקרבות הלבבות מה שלא יעלם וזה כי האדם לא יודיע פרטי עניניו כי אם לאוהבו ויעלימ׳ מהשונא וזה אם כן ממה שייסד בלבו שהוא אוהבו וישבר לבבו ותסור שנאתו ממנו ולזה תמצא ששלח יעקב מלאכים לעשו להודיע לו עניניו כדי שיתיישב בלבו שהוא אוהבו.

I n *Parashas Vayishlach*, Esav is coming to kill Yaakov with four hundred armed warriors. Yaakov prepares for the confrontation with three main strategies: Prayer to G-d, bribes to soften him up, and a strategy of dividing his camp into two so that if one gets destroyed, the other can escape.

> *Yaakov sends messengers ahead of him to Esav his brother, saying...* **"I have sojourned with Lavan** *and have lingered until now.* **I have acquired oxen and donkeys,** *flocks, servants, and maidservants, and I am sending to tell my lord to find favor in your eyes."* *(Bereishis 32:5–6)*

Q on the verse

The *Ralbag* is bothered by a question. Why is Yaakov relating his personal story to his estranged brother? "**I have sojourned with Lavan...I have acquired oxen and donkeys...**" These details seem pointless for Yaakov to share, especially when the two are on the brink of war. Is he also going to tell Esav what he ate for breakfast?

A of the commentator

He answers that Yaakov was closing the gap between them by telling Esav private information that one would not normally share with his adversary. In essence, he was saying, "I'm only telling you this because I want to be close with you." This has the tremendous power to melt the hatred between their hearts and bring about love between them.

Q on the commentator

This *Ralbag* is difficult to understand. We are not talking about two brothers who loved one another dearly and had a trivial disagreement. For decades, the evil Esav harbored hatred in his heart, dreaming of the many ways to execute his brother and his entire family. So deep was his hatred that it became embedded in his descendants as well. He was a known murderer, rapist, and thief. Perhaps this tool of persuasion works on normal people, but why did the brilliant Yaakov feel that it would work on his brother?

New insight

A powerful lesson in human psychology is learned from this *Ralbag*. In addition to Yaakov's three strategies to avoid a civil war, there is a fourth: Sharing personal details of your life can be incredibly effective towards pacifying your enemy. Yaakov sincerely wanted a better relationship with his brother, and Esav sensed that sincerity in his heart. As a result, the two mended a relationship that seemed broken beyond repair.

Lesson
for life

We sometimes have relationships we wish were better, yet the situation seems hopeless. Through this secret tool to win friends and influence people, we can change our reality. Let us open up genuinely to those we care about and mend even the most estranged relationships. Through this, we can build peace amongst our families and communities.

Window of Opportunity

Dedicated by Mr. and Mrs. Harold and Judith Mittel
in memory of their parents,
Mr. and Mrs. Paul and Ruth Mittel

בראשית לב:כג: וַיָּקָם בַּלַּיְלָה הוּא וַיִּקַּח אֶת שְׁתֵּי נָשָׁיו וְאֶת שְׁתֵּי שִׁפְחֹתָיו וְאֶת אַחַד עָשָׂר יְלָדָיו וַיַּעֲבֹר אֵת מַעֲבַר יַבֹּק:

רש"י: וְאֶת אַחַד עָשָׂר יְלָדָיו. וְדִינָה הֵיכָן הָיְתָה? נְתָנָהּ בְּתֵבָה וְנָעַל בְּפָנֶיהָ, שֶׁלֹּא יִתֵּן בָּהּ עֵשָׂו עֵינָיו, וּלְכָךְ נֶעֱנַשׁ יַעֲקֹב שֶׁמְּנָעָהּ מֵאָחִיו, שֶׁמָּא תַּחֲזִירֶנּוּ לַמּוּטָב, וְנָפְלָה בְּיַד שְׁכֶם. (בראשית רבה)

שפתי חכמים: וקשה דמאי שנא מלאה שהיו מעשי עשו שנואין והכתוב מזכירה לשבח, ולא נענשה אף על פי שהיתה מחזירתו למוטב ולמה נענש יעקב? ויש לומר דשאני לאה לפי שבאותו זמן היה רשע גמור, דלקח נשים על נשיו ועשה עבירות חמורות, ואי אפשר להחזירו למוטב לפיכך מזכירה לשבח, אבל עכשיו שנכמרו רחמיו על יעקב ונשקו בכל לבו, איכא למימר שמא תחזירנו למוטב. (נחלת יעקב)

39

P arashas *Vayishlach* describes Yaakov preparing for war with his evil twin, Esav, after having been separated for over two decades.

> *But he got up that night and took his two wives, his two handmaidens, **and his eleven sons**, and crossed the River Jabbok. (Bereishis 32:23)*

Rashi is bothered by a question. Why does the verse only mention "**his eleven sons**"? Where is his daughter, Dinah?

He answers that he hid her in a box so that the evil Esav would not be attracted to her. *Rashi* continues that because of Yaakov's mistake, he was later punished. The righteous Dinah could have changed Esav and influenced him to be much better had they gotten married, but now those hopes were dashed.

Sifsei Chachamim (who quotes *Nachalas Yaakov*) asks on *Rashi*: We know that Leah, Dinah's mother, was praised for doing everything in her power to avoid marrying the evil Esav because she would not have been able to effectuate change in him. So why was Yaakov faulted for hiding Dinah, when presumably she would not have been any more successful?

They answer that at this juncture in Esav's life, he temporarily melted his hatred and had compassion towards Yaakov, wanting to come closer to Yaakov and his family. At this climactic and emotional moment, had Esav seen Dinah, he could have changed his entire life for the good.

Most of our lives, we run around busying ourselves with things that are important to us. Once in a while, however, we can sense the fingerprints of divinity and become incredibly inspired to make real and lasting changes in our lives. Such moments, such opportunities pass quickly, and if we fail to seize them, we revert back to our "regular selves." When we are presented with that precious window of opportunity, we must grasp it before it vanishes.

The Finer Things in Life

לעילוי נשמת ר' נפתלי הערץ ב"ר מאיר ז"ל

בראשית לז:יב: וַיֵּלְכוּ אֶחָיו לִרְעוֹת אֶת צֹאן אֲבִיהֶם בִּשְׁכֶם:

רש"י: לרעות את צאן. נָקוּד עַל אֶת, שֶׁלֹּא הָלְכוּ אֶלָּא לִרְעוֹת אֶת עַצְמָן.

שפתי חכמים: נקוד על את שלא הלכו אלא לרעות את עצמן—"והוי פירושו הכי הלכו לרעות היינו את עצמן".

In *Parashas Vayeishev*, we learn about the intense jealousy that Yaakov's sons harbored towards their youngest brother, Yosef, because Yaakov favored him the most. The brothers set off for Shechem, and Yaakov asks Yosef to check on them.

*Now, his brothers went to **feed their father's flock** in Shechem. (Bereishis 37:12)*

The commentator explains *Rashi* (with *Sifsei Chachamim*) tells us that the Torah writes dots over the above bolded words, alluding to a hidden meaning that they did not just go to "**feed their father's flock**" but rather to feed themselves a fancy meal. At this very meal, they convened a Jewish court case against Yosef and concluded that they must do everything in their power to get rid of him since he was out to destroy them. Ultimately, this led them to sell Yosef into slavery to the Yishmaelim.

This *Rashi* is difficult to understand. If the brothers misjudged Yosef and were too harsh, then that is the problem. What does them having a fancy meal before the court case have to do with anything?

Rashi is teaching us that while they were taking care of themselves, they became slightly too engrossed in physicality, clouding their judgment on the case itself. Had they indulged less, they would have assessed Yosef's situation with greater clarity and would have come to an entirely different conclusion—one in which he was innocent.

It is great to enjoy wine, high-quality food, and the finer things in life. These delights are here for our benefit, and we should take advantage of them. In fact, one of the questions G-d will ask us "upstairs" after 120 years is if we enjoyed His world. Like everything in life, however, there is a balance. Appreciating physicality is one thing, but becoming steeped in it is quite another. We should always enjoy—in moderation—what the world has to offer in order to maintain our mental clarity and judgment.

Living with Dignity

בראשית לז:כה: וַיֵּשְׁבוּ לֶאֱכָל לֶחֶם וַיִּשְׂאוּ עֵינֵיהֶם וַיִּרְאוּ וְהִנֵּה אֹרְחַת יִשְׁמְעֵאלִים בָּאָה מִגִּלְעָד וּגְמַלֵּיהֶם נֹשְׂאִים נְכֹאת וּצְרִי וָלֹט הוֹלְכִים לְהוֹרִיד מִצְרָיְמָה:

רלב״ג: התועלת השמיני הוא בדעות. והוא להודיע עוצם השגחת השי״ת בטובים עד שכבר סבב הש׳ יתע׳ כשהביא ההכרח שימכר יוסף להצילו מהמות שיהיה נמכר לנכבדים נושאם סחורות נכבדות וחמודות וסבב גם כן שמכרוהו לשר נכבד בארץ מצרים כי העבודה לנכבדים אין בה מהקושי והצער כמו שהיה מזה בעבודה לפחותים וזה מבואר בנפשו.

In *Parashas Vayeishev*, Yosef's brothers turn against him, fueled by jealousy that their father favors him the most. The brothers devise a plan to kill him, but change their minds at the last minute and sell Yosef to Yishmaelim who happen to be passing by.

43

> *A caravan of Yishmaelim was coming from Gilad, their*
> *camels bearing spices, balsam, and lotus—on their*
> *way to bring them down to Egypt. (Bereishis 37:25)*

Yosef is ultimately sold into slavery to work for Potiphar, a high-ranking officer in Pharaoh's palace.

The commentator explains

The *Ralbag* tells us that G-d orchestrated every step of Yosef's journey to ensure that he was always surrounded by prominent people. From the very beginning, he was transported to Egypt in a caravan of high-class merchants carrying aromatic spices, when normally caravans with foul-smelling cargo traversed that route. Once in Egypt, he was made a slave to one of Pharaoh's top ministers. These details made Yosef's fate much more bearable, allowing him to retain his dignity and self-worth.

Q on the commentator

This seems puzzling. If someone is sold into slavery, why should it matter if he is working for the upper, middle, or lower class? In any case, a slave is a slave and is subject to the will of his master. That alone is enough to erode a person's spirit.

New insight

This *Ralbag* teaches an amazing lesson in human psychology. When Yosef found himself working for these special people, he felt better about himself, his dignity, and what he stood for. Although still a slave who did not own anything or make decisions for himself, he could convince himself that he was making a difference in the world by running the office of a high government official.

Lesson for life

We can tap into our highest selves by emulating G-d. Let us take note of G-d's extra care for the details of Yosef's journey to protect his self-worth. We too can improve the lives of those around us by making the effort to treat them with an extra level of respect and dignity.

MIKEITZ

Do Appearances
Really Matter?

Dedicated by the Aqua Family in memory
of their grandparents Sydney Joseph (שמאי יוסף)
and Marjorie (מרים) Silberman

בראשית מא:יד: וַיִּשְׁלַח פַּרְעֹה וַיִּקְרָא אֶת יוֹסֵף וַיְרִיצֻהוּ מִן הַבּוֹר
וַיְגַלַּח וַיְחַלֵּף שִׂמְלֹתָיו וַיָּבֹא אֶל פַּרְעֹה:

רלב"ג: התועלת הראשון הוא במדות. והוא להודיע שראוי לאדם
בבאו לפני הגדולים שיקשט עצמו בבגדיו ובענייניו האחרים לפי
מה שאפשר כי בזה מהההדור לגדולים ובזה גם כן יהיו דבריו
יותר נשמעים. ולזה תמצא שגלח יוסף והחליף שמלותיו בבאו
לפני המלך.

I n *Parashas Mikeitz*, Pharaoh is troubled by recurring dreams
and calls upon his advisors for help interpreting them, but
no one can correctly interpret them. The royal butler informs
Pharaoh that there is a prisoner, Yosef, who is a skilled dream
interpreter, and Pharaoh sends for him immediately.

45

> *So, Pharaoh sent and summoned Yosef, and they rushed him from the dungeon. He shaved and changed his clothes, and he came to Pharaoh. (Bereishis 41:14)*

The commentator explains

The *Ralbag* explains that Yosef was given a shave, haircut, and new clothing designed by royal tailors not only to show respect before the king, but because "had they whisked him straight to Pharaoh in his current condition, Pharaoh wouldn't have fully listened to him."

Q on the commentator

This *Ralbag* begs the question. Why would Pharaoh not listen to Yosef simply because of his disheveled appearance? He had been losing sleep over obscure dreams, and Yosef is an expert interpreter who could finally bring him peace of mind. What difference would it make if Yosef appeared with long hair, a beard, and chains around his neck?

New insight

The *Ralbag* is teaching us that although Pharaoh was eager to hear what Yosef had to say, he wouldn't be able to look past Yosef's unkempt state. Once Yosef was dressed appropriately, Pharaoh would listen to him, even though Pharaoh knew that this is the same inmate who looked quite different just a few hours ago. For this reason, they made Yosef an appointment with the royal barber and tailor, and only then would Pharaoh truly appreciate all he would say. Ultimately, Yosef's interpretation of the dreams saved much of the world from starvation, as he warned Pharaoh to prepare for an impending famine.

Lesson for life

As we go about our daily lives, we often feel that if we do not wear a tie, fix our hair, or clean up our office, the people with whom we come in contact will look beyond these trivial, superficial things and, instead, focus on what is truly important. Although in a perfect world that should be the case, it almost never is. Let us present ourselves in a dignified manner that reflects our true values and the messages we want to convey.

Hitting Rock Bottom

Dedicated by the Aqua family
in memory of their grandmother Yonah (חממה)
and in honor of their grandfather Saadya (סעדיה) Aqua

בראשית מב:לז: וַיֹּאמֶר רְאוּבֵן אֶל אָבִיו לֵאמֹר אֶת שְׁנֵי בָנַי תָּמִית אִם לֹא אֲבִיאֶנּוּ אֵלֶיךָ תְּנָה אֹתוֹ עַל יָדִי וַאֲנִי אֲשִׁיבֶנּוּ אֵלֶיךָ:

רמב"ן: את שני בני תמית והכלל כי היתה עצת יהודה טובה להניחו לזקן עד שיכלה פת מן הבית (עיין תנחומא מקץ ח) כי אז ישמע והוא מה שאמר לו ונחיה ולא נמות גם אנחנו גם טפנו.

In *Parashas Mikeitz*, the Torah records a conversation between Yaakov and his sons regarding their inability to appear again before the viceroy of Egypt if they are not accompanied by their brother, Binyamin. On a previous visit to Egypt, the viceroy, having learned about their youngest brother, demanded that the brothers bring Binyamin on their next visit or he would no longer provide them with food during the worldwide famine.

> *Then Reuven told his father, "You may slay my two sons if I fail to bring him back to you. Put him in my care, and I will return him to you." (Bereishis 42:37)*

Yaakov refuses his offer. A few verses later, Yehudah tries again to convince Yaakov and is successful.

Q on the verse *Ramban* is bothered by a question. Why did Yehudah succeed, whereas Reuven had failed?

A of the commentator He answers that Yehudah had a brilliant idea to wait a short time longer to approach his father until the food supply ran out, and only then did he try to persuade Yaakov to send Binyamin.

Q on the commentator This *Ramban* is puzzling! Why couldn't Yehudah have stepped up immediately after Reuven's failure with the following idea: "Dad, we're running extremely low on food during a harsh famine. The only food left is in Egypt. Soon our provisions will run out, and we would not want you, your children, or grandchildren to starve." Couldn't the wise Yaakov understand that the family was in dire straits and needed to act immediately?

New insight The *Ramban* is teaching us an insight into human nature. Had Yehudah stepped up right then and there, Yaakov would not have listened to him because, for the time being, there was still food in the fridge and the pantry. Although intellectually Yaakov knew that they would run out very soon, they had not hit rock bottom. Therefore, Yehudah understood that Yaakov was not yet ready emotionally to digest this message.

Lesson for life When we try to help others, we often do it on our own schedule and with our own agenda. We mean well, but if the other person is not ready to hear what we have to offer, we will not be effective in assisting him. Let us be attuned to the needs of others and be ready to assist them at the appropriate time.

VAYIGASH

All in the Family

Dedicated by Joseph and Michelle Sherman in memory
of their grandparents Larry and Yetta Sherman

בראשית מה:טז: וְהַקֹּל נִשְׁמַע בֵּית פַּרְעֹה לֵאמֹר בָּאוּ אֲחֵי יוֹסֵף
וַיִּיטַב בְּעֵינֵי פַרְעֹה וּבְעֵינֵי עֲבָדָיו:

ספורנו: וייטב בעיני פרעה שחשב שמכאן ואילך תהיה השגחת
יוסף על הארץ לא כהשגחת גר מנהיג אבל כהשגחת אזרח.
חושב לשבת בארץ הוא וזרעו ולזה ישגיח בכל לב להטיב לארץ
וליושביה.

In *Parashas Vayigash*, word reached the Egyptian people that
Yosef's entire family was moving to town.

> The news was heard in Pharaoh's palace saying,
> "Yosef's brothers have come!" And it was pleasing in
> the eyes of Pharaoh and in the eyes of his servants.
> (Bereishis 45:16)

49

Q on the verse
The *Sforno* is bothered by a question: Why does the Torah need to mention their reactions? Isn't it obvious everyone would be happy for Yosef? What lesson is to be learned here?

A of the commentator
He answers: "From here on out, Yosef will run Egypt with his best efforts as one who has his family around, not as a stranger living in a land alone and away from his beloved family."

Q on the commentator
This *Sforno* is hard to understand. It implies that the job done by Yosef was subpar until this point and that only now would he give it his all. We know that Yosef interpreted the dreams of Pharaoh to mean seven robust years followed by seven years of worldwide famine. He was then put in charge of storing the food and creating a system to save millions of people from starvation. He was honest, hard-working, humble, and treated everyone with respect. There was no one who questioned his work ethic. He wasn't taking several coffee breaks a day. What does this *Sforno* mean?

New insight
We learn from this *Sforno* just how important family can be. Without them, Yosef was among the top CEOs of his time. He was second-in-command of the most successful country in the world. Despite all of this, however, Yosef had the potential to be even more productive with the love and support of his family living near him.

Lesson for life
During these unprecedented times, we may have seen our family only sparingly or not at all. Regardless, they love us and give us support more than anyone. We should be as creative as possible to make sure we Zoom, Facetime, or visit those loved ones who will not only appreciate the effort but will make us better people as well.

Honoring the Office

Dedicated by Joseph and Michelle Sherman in memory
of their grandparents Jules and Ruth Kent

בראשית מה:כב–כג: לְכֻלָּם נָתַן לָאִישׁ חֲלִפוֹת שְׂמָלֹת וּלְבִנְיָמִן
נָתַן שְׁלֹשׁ מֵאוֹת כֶּסֶף וְחָמֵשׁ חֲלִפֹת שְׂמָלֹת: וּלְאָבִיו שָׁלַח כְּזֹאת
עֲשָׂרָה חֲמֹרִים נֹשְׂאִים מִטּוּב מִצְרָיִם וְעֶשֶׂר אֲתֹנֹת נֹשְׂאֹת בָּר וָלֶחֶם
וּמָזוֹן לְאָבִיו לַדָּרֶךְ:

רלב״ג: התועלת הה׳ הוא במדות. והוא שראוי לאדם כשישתדל
בדבר מה להשתדל׳ להסיר כל מונע שימנעהו מהשיג מבוקשו
ולהראות כל אשר מביא יביאהו להשיגו. ולזה תמצא כי מפני
שהיה יוסף יודע שיעקב מתירא מההעתק מארץ כנען להיותה
הארץ הנבחרת ומיראת ממשלת מצרים שהיתה קשה מאד
הודיע אותו כי יש לו ממשלה עצומה בארץ מצרים לעשות כל
מה שירצה ולזה לא יירא לבא למצרים כי כשירצה לשוב יוכל
לשוב עם שכבר יהיה זה סבה שלא יורש הוא וביתו ברעב כמו
שזכר ושלח לו עם זה דורון נפלא להראותו עשרו ויכולתו ועוצם
רצונו להטיב לו ושלח לו ג״כ מהבגדים החמודים כדי שיתרצה
יעקב יותר לבא שם ולא ימנע יעקב מלבא שם מפני שאינם
מלובשים בגדים חמודות כראוי להתראות לפני המלך באופן

51

שלא יהיו נבזים בעיניו וימתין עד קנותו אותם ולזה שלח לו
מהבגדים החמודות מה ששלח.

In *Parashas Vayigash*, after having been separated for twenty-two years, Yosef shocks his brothers by revealing his identity as none other than the viceroy of Egypt. His miraculous rise to prominence placed him only second in the ranks to Pharaoh, overseeing the entire food distribution during the famine. He urges his brothers to bring their father Yaakov to live in Egypt so Yosef can provide for the entire family.

> To each of the brothers, he gave changes of clothing,
> but to Binyamin he gave three hundred pieces of silver
> and five changes of clothing. And to his father he gave
> **like this** [clothing for him, his wives, and the young
> children]...(Bereishis 45:22–23)

The commentator explains — The *Ralbag* explains that Yosef made sure to send Yaakov fine and distinguished clothing befitting of one who is visiting a king so that Yaakov should not delay his move to Egypt.

Q on the commentator — This begs the question: Yaakov was told over two decades ago that his favorite son Yosef was killed in a freak accident. Now he finds out that not only is he alive and well, but he is in a position to help Yaakov's entire family during the worst economic calamity in the history of the world. Wouldn't we expect Yaakov to run and call the movers at his first opportunity? Would Yaakov really delay getting to Egypt to see his long-lost son because he lacked the right clothing?

New insight — The *Ralbag* teaches us a spectacular lesson. As motivated as Yaakov was to see his son after all these years apart, Yosef knew that his father would not come unless he was prepared appropriately. Even though Yaakov had nice clothing, and people would surely understand there was no Amazon Prime for royal clothing, Yaakov felt it was not suitable for him to show up until he was properly attired to show respect to the office of the king.

Lesson
for life There are countless examples in *Sefer Shemos* where Moshe and Aharon are directed to show respect to the Office of Pharaoh. One may ask why it was necessary to show respect to an evil dictator who oppressed the Jews. But we see that G-d tells us that if He places a particular person in charge, there is a reason behind it, and we must respect the people who hold positions of prominence—even if we do not endorse what they represent.

We may not support various figures who hold positions of power, but the Torah teaches us that nonetheless, we must show proper honor to them and be a *mensch*. This is not because of who they are as people, but because of the positions that they hold.

VAYECHI

The Power of Appreciation

Dedicated by Michael and Sylvia Kanoff and Family
(Miami Beach, FL)
in memory of Esther Kanoff (Yahrtzeit 8 Av)

בראשית מז:כח: וַיְחִי יַעֲקֹב בְּאֶרֶץ מִצְרַיִם שְׁבַע עֶשְׂרֵה שָׁנָה וַיְהִי יְמֵי יַעֲקֹב שְׁנֵי חַיָּיו שֶׁבַע שָׁנִים וְאַרְבָּעִים וּמְאַת שָׁנָה:

דעת זקנים: ויחי יעקב בארץ מצרים. למה הזכיר הכתוב סך חייו בארץ מצרים לפי שמצינו שיוסף הי' עם אביו קודם מכירתו י"ז שנה וכשם שפרנס יעקב ליוסף י"ז שנה כך יוסף פרנסו וכלכלו י"ז שנה כנגדן הה"ד אלה תולדות יעקב יוסף בן שבע עשרה שנה.

חזקוני: מקרא זה נכתב לשבחו של יוסף, שפרנס את אביו ואת כל בני ביתו י"ז שנה, כמו שפרנסו אביו, שהרי בן י"ז שנה היה כשנמכר.

54

P *arashas Vayechi* describes the final years of Yaakov's life:

> *Yaakov lived in the land of Egypt* **seventeen years***; and the days of Yaakov—the years of his life—were* **147 years***. (Bereishis 47:28)*

Q on the verse *Daas Zekeinim* and *Chizkuni* are bothered by a question. The Torah previously tells us that Yaakov moved down to Egypt at **130 years of age**, so why does it state that he died at **147** and that he lived there for **17 years**? Can't we do basic math to figure out how many years he lived in Egypt?

A of the commentator They answer that the Torah is not just telling us a fact but emphasizing the greatness of Yosef for taking care of his father Yaakov (and his entire household) for seventeen years, just like Yaakov had cared for Yosef for seventeen years before he left home.

Q on the commentator There are three problems with *Daas Zekeinim* and *Chizkuni*'s insight:

1. Why is the Torah praising Yosef the Righteous for doing what anyone would do for his parents? Yosef had access to food, and his father did not. Wouldn't anyone do what he did?
2. Had Yosef's father lived eighteen years, would Yosef have said to his father, "I'm sorry, but I'm not supporting you further because you only took care of me for seventeen years?" Surely not.
3. If Yosef was taking care of his father in repayment of what was done for him, why did he take care of *his entire household* as well?

New insight The answer is that the Torah is not praising Yosef for something any child would do. Of course, Yosef would have supported Yaakov for longer if needed. Instead, the Torah is singling out the exceptional quality of how Yosef treated his father for these seventeen years: in the same manner his father lovingly took care of him. His enthusiasm never wavered, constantly reminding himself of the amazing opportunity that he had to take care of all his father's needs, which included his entire household as well.

Lesson for life   The obligation of *hakaras hatov* (gratitude) is a fundamental part of the Torah. We should always strive to do *chessed* (kindness) for each other because it is the right thing to do. If we are on the receiving end of that kindness, we should feel it deeply and look for opportunities to help in return. Parents, teachers, friends, and colleagues have all helped us numerous times. If we internalize their *chessed* and truly appreciate it, it will propel us to reciprocate with an enthusiasm that we never knew was possible!

How to Talk
So You'll Be Heard

Dedicated by Michael and Sylvia Kanoff and Family
(Miami Beach, FL)
in memory of Esther Kanoff (Yahrtzeit 8 Av)

בראשית מח:ז: וַאֲנִי בְּבֹאִי מִפַּדָּן מֵתָה עָלַי רָחֵל בְּאֶרֶץ כְּנַעַן בַּדֶּרֶךְ בְּעוֹד כִּבְרַת אֶרֶץ לָבֹא אֶפְרָתָה וָאֶקְבְּרֶהָ שָּׁם בְּדֶרֶךְ אֶפְרָת הִוא בֵּית לָחֶם:

חזקוני: לכך קברה שם יעקב לפי שגנות הוא לאשה מתה יולדת להוליכה למרחוק ולהשהותה פן יהיו דמיה מלכלכים תכריכיה. ולפי שרצה להקבר בארץ כנען הזכיר ליוסף זאת שלא יאשימהו על אמו ולא יהיה עצל בדבר.

In *Parashas Vayechi*, Yaakov calls for Yosef to visit, as he is nearing the end of his life. He asks Yosef to ensure that he has a kosher burial in the Land of Israel.

Yaakov now relates to Yosef the details of his mother Rachel's burial—a seemingly unrelated discussion:

"But as for me—when I came from Paddan, Rachel died on me in the land of Canaan on the road while there was still a stretch of land to go to Ephrat; and I buried her there on the road to Ephrat, which is Beis Lechem." (Bereishis 48:7)

The commentator explains

Chizkuni explains that had Yaakov not related the details of the extenuating circumstances obstructing Rachel from getting a proper funeral, Yosef would have been lax on some level when carrying out his last wishes.

Q on the commentator

This is mystifying. Yosef loved his father dearly and was eager to do everything in his power to help him. Why couldn't Yaakov just tell Yosef there was an uncontrollable situation that caused him to bury Rachel where he did, without giving any further explanation?

New insight

From this *Chizkuni*, we glean an insight into the human psyche. While it is true that Yosef would have followed through to fulfill his dad's request, he would not have given it 100 percent until he felt that he clearly understood the scenario surrounding his mother's burial. Only being armed with this knowledge would he fully commit himself to Yaakov's burial.

Lesson for life

One of things we remember most from our childhood is asking an adult why we cannot do something, only to receive the response, "Because I said so." While we may trust intuitively that the parent or teacher has our best interests in mind, we cannot fully appreciate their decisions until we are given the rationale behind it. As we grow up, we do not cherish hearing those words any more than we did as a child. Although at times we are not able to divulge every detail, we should realize that the more we can explain, the more likely our kids, staff, and those around us will feel motivated to help us or comply with our wishes.

Sefer Shemos

In honor of our parents
Leiby and Aidy Schonfeld
and ## Shloime and Esther Werdiger
And in honor of our children
Ilana and Ozzie Fischer
Abie and Pessi Genack
Riki, Moshe and Rosie

Avromi and Shoshana Schonfeld

The True Value of a Dollar

Dedicated by Sheila Hecker in memory
of Harvey Hecker, Chaim Yissochar ben Yechiel V'Sara

שמות ב:ג: וְלֹא יָכְלָה עוֹד הַצְּפִינוֹ וַתִּקַּח לוֹ תֵּבַת גֹּמֶא וַתַּחְמְרָה
בַחֵמָר וּבַזָּפֶת וַתָּשֶׂם בָּהּ אֶת הַיֶּלֶד וַתָּשֶׂם בַּסּוּף עַל שְׂפַת הַיְאֹר:

דעת זקנים: תיבת גומא. לפי שהוא דומה לסוף שעל שפת היאור
ולא יכירו בו האויבים בסוטה מסיק מכאן לצדיקים שממונם חביב
עליהם יותר מגופם וכל כך למה לפי שאין פושטין ידם בגזל.

Parashas *Shemos* relates that the Egyptians began to enslave the Jewish People, and the astronomers of Pharaoh foretell that soon the Jewish redeemer will be born. Pharaoh then issues an edict that all Jewish boys born should be thrown into the Nile River.

Moshe was born as a preemie at only six months. As a result, his mother, Yocheved, was able to easily hide his birth from the authorities for three months, after which she had to be creative to save his life.

61

She could not hide him any longer, so she took for him
*a **wicker basket** and smeared it with clay and pitch;*
she placed the boy into it and placed it among the reeds
at the bank of the River. (Shemos 2:3)

Q on the verse The *Daas Zekeinim* is bothered by a question. We know that Yocheved had gone to great lengths camouflaging his basket to blend into the Nile's surroundings. Why then wouldn't she expend a little more time, effort, and energy to place him in a sturdier wooden basket that would be more likely to help save him?

A of the commentator He quotes Rabbi Eliezer from the Talmud (*Sotah* 12a), who teaches that although a wooden basket would have been better, the righteous Yocheved was concerned about using pricier material and chose to use the cheaper straw version of the basket instead. *Daas Zekeinim* concludes, "This is commendable so that the righteous will never end up stealing."

Q on the commentator How can we understand this *Daas Zekeinim*? Yocheved was a highly devoted mother who cared deeply for her child and worried that he might die. Wouldn't she go to great lengths to do a little more for her child, even spending more money on his bassinet? And what does the choice of material used in the basket have to do with the possibility of ending up stealing?

New insight The *Daas Zekeinim* is teaching that while Yocheved did so much in attempting to save her child, she did so with her eye on the big picture. She knew she had to do her best and, hopefully, G-d would do the rest to save baby Moshe. She understood that squandering money would be considered excessive and unnecessary by G-d. Yocheved also appreciated that if one is wasteful with her money, she can one day land in the poorhouse, tempted to steal to sustain herself.

Lesson for life Money is a big focus of our lives, and for good reason; without it, we have nothing to wear or eat and will not survive. The Torah shows us the true value of a dollar. We are instructed to appreciate what is entrusted to us and make the best use of it for ourselves and for others who are less fortunate. Even when using this wonderful asset to help others, the Torah directs us to be cautious when contributing to charity, lest we become impoverished ourselves. Let us treasure what G-d has deposited in our accounts and use it for the proper causes while striking the balance to keep us on solid ground.

Seeing Is Believing!

*Dedicated by Sheila Hecker in memory
of Harvey Hecker, Chaim Yissochar ben Yechiel V'Sara*

שמות ג:יב: וַיֹּאמֶר כִּי אֶהְיֶה עִמָּךְ וְזֶה לְּךָ הָאוֹת כִּי אָנֹכִי שְׁלַחְתִּיךָ
בְּהוֹצִיאֲךָ אֶת הָעָם מִמִּצְרַיִם תַּעַבְדוּן אֶת הָאֱלֹקִים עַל הָהָר הַזֶּה:

רש"י: וַיֹּאמֶר כי אהיה עמך. וזה הַמַּרְאֶה אֲשֶׁר רָאִיתָ בַּסְּנֶה לְךָ
הָאוֹת כִּי אָנֹכִי שְׁלַחְתִּיךָ, וְתַצְלִיחַ בִּשְׁלִיחוּתִי וּכְדַאי אֲנִי לְהַצִּיל,
כַּאֲשֶׁר רָאִיתָ הַסְּנֶה עוֹשֶׂה שְׁלִיחוּתִי וְאֵינֶנּוּ אֻכָּל, כָּךְ תֵּלֵךְ
בִּשְׁלִיחוּתִי וְאֵינְךָ נִזּוֹק.

שפתי חכמים: כך תלך בשליחותי ואינך ניזוק. דאם לא כן, לך
למה לי. אלא לך לך האות שאין אתה ניזוק כשתלך בשליחותי,
כאשר ראית הסנה שאינו אכל. ודו"ק.

In *Parashas Shemos*, G-d appears to Moshe in a miraculous burning bush that does not get burned. Moshe then asks G-d to protect him from Pharaoh when requesting to release the Jews from bondage in Egypt, and G-d assures him:

> "For I shall be with you—and this is your sign that
> I have sent you." (Shemos 3:12)

The commentator explains

Rashi (with *Sifsei Chachamim*) tells us that G-d addressed Moshe's concern for his safety by displaying the burning bush. G-d was telling Moshe, "Just as you see the burning bush is carrying out my will and it isn't being consumed, so too, if you do as I ask, I will protect you so that the evil Pharaoh will not harm you."

Q on the commentator

This begs the question: Why can't G-d just tell Moshe that He will protect him without any visual effects?

New insight

Rashi and *Sifsei Chachamim* are teaching us an amazing lesson. Once Hashem pointed out that the miraculous spectacle was a metaphor for His protection, the imagery had a powerful effect on Moshe. If Moshe only heard from the voice of G-d that he would be protected, it would not penetrate his whole being as deeply as seeing a live demonstration of the protection that Hashem provides for those who serve him. Something tangible has the deepest impression on a person.

Lesson for life

There is a famous Torah axiom: "You can't compare hearing to seeing." We may know an idea intellectually, but seeing and experiencing it brings a whole new level of understanding and appreciation.

We may understand that G-d created the world and runs it, but we do not fully internalize this fact by just knowing it. One of the best ways to experience the reality of G-d is through miracles in nature. From a tiny hard seed grows a beautiful orange tree that reaps fruit every year, and its aromatic peel protects it from the elements and spoilage. The tiniest creatures, such as ants, can somehow thrive and carry many times their own weight. Let us open our eyes and recognize that Hashem's signature is on everything around us, and let us utilize such observations to form a stronger bond with Him.

VA'EIRA

Effective Speaking

---

*Dedicated by Marc and Phyllis Beresin in loving
dedication to their parents Leo and Anne Beresin*

שמות ו:ט: וַיְדַבֵּר מֹשֶׁה כֵּן אֶל בְּנֵי יִשְׂרָאֵל וְלֹא שָׁמְעוּ אֶל מֹשֶׁה
מִקֹּצֶר רוּחַ וּמֵעֲבֹדָה קָשָׁה:

רלב"ג: התועלת הרביעי הוא במדות. והוא שראוי לאדם כשירצה
ולהשיג דבר מה מהאנשים שיסדר דבריו בתכלית מה שאפשר
לסדר בהם מלקיחת הנפשות למה שירצהו ומיפוי הדברים ההם
וקשוטם כדי שיפותו לשמוע אליו כי בזולת זה אפשר שלא ישיג
מבוקשו ואף על פי שיהיו הדברים ההם להגיע תועלת להם. הלא
תראה כי זה המאמר' שהיה מצווה משם שיאמר לישר' עם רוב
מה שיש בענינו מהטוב להם ומהפתוי אל שיאמינו בדברים ההם
הנה לא שמעו ישראל אל משה מפני קוצר רוחו משה מלהשתדל
לסדר דבריו באופן שלם בדרך שיפותו להאמין לדבריו.

In *Parashas Va'eira*, Moshe tries to reassure the Jewish People
that they will be freed from slavery, but they pay little attention to him.

66

So Moshe spoke accordingly to the Children of Israel;
*but they did not heed Moshe, **because of shortness of***
***breath** and hard work. (Shemos 6:9)*

Q on the verse — The *Ralbag* is bothered by a question. They had vetted Moshe's credentials as their savior and were eager to be freed after hundreds of years of slavery. So, what does it mean, "...they did not heed Moshe **because of shortness of breath**"?

A of the commentator — He answers that although they verified Moshe through his family, his prophecy, and display of miracles, the Jews just could not digest his words fully. Why? Because when Moshe spoke to them about G-d redeeming them now, on some level his delivery was lacking. The words were coming out, but they were not hitting their mark.

Q on the commentator — This *Ralbag* is bewildering! The only factors at play here should be the "who" and "what." Moshe is for real, and they are determined to "get out of Dodge." Nothing else should matter—not his delivery, his vocabulary, or his speaking skills!

New insight — We learn from this *Ralbag* an incredible lesson about speaking in a manner that people will listen. Although the content and person delivering the message should mean everything, sometimes one's oratory skills and delivery make all the difference in the world. Had Moshe spent a little more time on those factors, he would have been effective immediately.

Lesson for life — While it is true that the most important element of a message is the content, it is vital to organize our thoughts and deliver them in a way that is polished, persuasive, and cogent. Let us invest time and energy into both our ideas and an effective delivery so that we have the power to truly impact others with our words.

Blinded from Reality

Dedicated by Marc and Phyllis Beresin in loving dedication to their parents Larry and Ida Garber

שמות ט:ל–לב: וְאַתָּה וַעֲבָדֶיךָ יָדַעְתִּי כִּי טֶרֶם תִּירְאוּן מִפְּנֵי ה'
אֱלֹקִים: וְהַפִּשְׁתָּה וְהַשְּׂעֹרָה נֻכָּתָה כִּי הַשְּׂעֹרָה אָבִיב וְהַפִּשְׁתָּה גִּבְעֹל:
וְהַחִטָּה וְהַכֻּסֶּמֶת לֹא נֻכּוּ כִּי אֲפִילֹת הֵנָּה:

חזקוני: ידעתי כי טרם תיראון עדין אינכם יראים שהרי החטה
והכוסמת לא נכו ועדיין יש לכם לאכול.

In *Parashas Va'eira*, the Torah describes how the plague of hail was a miraculous mixture of fire and ice, pelting the ground, and as the ice broke apart, the fire escaped and consumed most of the crops.

Moshe admonishes Pharaoh:

> *"And as for you and your servants, I know that you are not yet afraid of G-d. The flax and the barley were struck, for the barley was ripe and the flax was in its stalk. And **the wheat and the spelt were not struck, they will ripen later.**" (Shemos 9:30–32)*

Q on the verse *Chizkuni* asks, how is it possible that the Egyptians were not afraid of G-d after experiencing the majority of the plagues?

A of the commentator He answers that although they had suffered great losses, since **"the wheat and the spelt were not struck"** by hail, they still had food to eat and felt complacent.

Q on the commentator The *Chizkuni's* insight into the Egyptians' reaction is incomprehensible. They had experienced plagues for months, which had caused fish and animals to die. Lice, boils, and frogs caused tremendous physical discomfort and hysteria. The vast crops were nearly annihilated. And now, since they had a little unripe wheat and spelt, they felt secure and still stood defiant against G-d and Moshe. That sounds ridiculous!

New insight We learn from this *Chizkuni* an important lesson in human nature. Pharaoh and his people were anti-Semitic slave owners who did not want to change their ways. They did not want to let the Jewish People go, and no matter what G-d threw at them, they remained steadfast in their commitment. They would latch onto the smallest thing to maintain their beliefs and way of life, ignoring reality for as long as they could.

Lesson for life Our beliefs, value systems, and upbringing can cloud our judgment and blind us from seeing objectively. We are hard-wired to feel that our way of thinking is correct. By delving into the Torah, we can navigate the "waters of life" through G-d's prism of clarity for anything that comes our way. We can also seek guidance from those who are not steeped in our issues and can therefore see more clearly. Through these ways, we can arrive at the truth and actualize our potential.

BO

The Majesty of Man

Dedicated by Rabbi Shimon and Nechama Feder
in honor of their parents
Rabbi and Mrs. Larry and Elizabeth Feder
and Mr. and Mrs. Harold and Judith Mittel

שמות י״א:ה׳: וּמֵת כָּל בְּכוֹר בְּאֶרֶץ מִצְרַיִם מִבְּכוֹר פַּרְעֹה הַיֹּשֵׁב עַל
כִּסְאוֹ עַד בְּכוֹר הַשִּׁפְחָה אֲשֶׁר אַחַר הָרֵחָיִם וְכֹל בְּכוֹר בְּהֵמָה:

שמות י״ב:ב׳:כ״ט: וַיְהִי בַּחֲצִי הַלַּיְלָה וַה׳ הִכָּה כָל בְּכוֹר בְּאֶרֶץ מִצְרַיִם
מִבְּכֹר פַּרְעֹה הַיֹּשֵׁב עַל כִּסְאוֹ עַד בְּכוֹר הַשְּׁבִי אֲשֶׁר בְּבֵית הַבּוֹר
וְכֹל בְּכוֹר בְּהֵמָה:

חזקוני: ומת כל בכור שמחו בכורי השפחה אמרו עכשו לא
יהיה חלוק בינינו ובין אדונינו כשראו אדוניהם ששמחו במפלתם
אסרו אותם בבור, ובאה עליהם המכה בעודם בבור נמצא בשעת
התראה בכור השפחה ובשעת המכה בכור השבי.

I n *Parashas Bo*, Moshe warns Pharaoh that G-d will soon wipe
out every Egyptian firstborn son.

"Every firstborn in the land of Egypt shall die, from the firstborn of Pharaoh who sits on his throne, to the **firstborn of the maidservant who is behind the millstone**." (Shemos 11:5)

Later, when the plague occurs, the Torah states:

It was at midnight that Hashem smote every firstborn in the land of Egypt, from the firstborn of Pharaoh sitting on his throne, to the **firstborn of the captive who was in the dungeon**. (Shemos 12:29)

Q on the verse

The *Chizkuni* asks, why does the verse switch? Originally, when Moshe warned them, he said, "from Pharaoh to the firstborn of the **maidservant who is behind the millstone**." When the plague actually happened, however, the Torah said, "from Pharaoh to the firstborn of the **captive who was in the dungeon**."

A of the commentator

He answers that when Moshe announced the plague, the servants rejoiced because they would finally be on the same level as their masters by receiving the same fate. Their masters saw them rejoicing at their expense and threw them into a dungeon. Therefore, these servants who were originally behind the millstone ended up in the dungeon!

Q on the commentator

This *Chizkuni* is astounding. While we may understand the servants' excitement over being on par with their masters for the first time of their lives, let's take a look at what we're talking about here. We are discussing their impending death. They would no longer be able to *schmooze* with friends, hang out with relatives, or enjoy the finer things in life. They would be dead. So why the exhilaration?

New insight

We learn from this *Chizkuni* a surprising insight into human psychology. The oppressed servants always craved respect along with their masters, so much so that when they heard they would be equal with them for the first time, they celebrated.

This deep-seated need for dignity overshadowed their feeling of self-preservation.

Lesson for life The majesty of man is that we long for respect, dignity, and self-worth. One of the greatest gifts we can give someone else is to show him his value and importance. Let us uplift those around us by recognizing their special qualities.

Peace and Tranquility

*Dedicated by Rabbi Shimon and Nechama Feder
in honor of their children Moshe, Riva, Malka,
Avraham, Adina, and Rusi*

שמות יב:לט: וַיֹּאפוּ אֶת הַבָּצֵק אֲשֶׁר הוֹצִיאוּ מִמִּצְרַיִם עֻגֹת מַצּוֹת
כִּי לֹא חָמֵץ כִּי גֹרְשׁוּ מִמִּצְרַיִם וְלֹא יָכְלוּ לְהִתְמַהְמֵהַּ וְגַם צֵדָה לֹא
עָשׂוּ לָהֶם:

רש"י: וגם צדה לא עשו להם. לַדֶּרֶךְ. מַגִּיד שִׁבְחָן שֶׁל יִשְׂרָאֵל,
שֶׁלֹּא אָמְרוּ הֵיאַךְ נֵצֵא לַמִּדְבָּר בְּלֹא צֵידָה? אֶלָּא הֶאֱמִינוּ וְהָלְכוּ;
הוּא שֶׁמְפֹרָשׁ בַּקַּבָּלָה, "זָכַרְתִּי לָךְ חֶסֶד נְעוּרַיִךְ אַהֲבַת כְּלוּלֹתָיִךְ
לֶכְתֵּךְ אַחֲרַי בַּמִּדְבָּר בְּאֶרֶץ לֹא זְרוּעָה". (ירמיהו ב')

In *Parashas Bo*, we begin the next chapter of the Jewish People as they are leaving Egypt and headed toward the desert as free men.

> *They baked the dough that they took out of Egypt into unleavened cakes, for they could not be leavened, for they were driven from Egypt for they could not*

*delay, **nor had they made provisions for themselves.*** *(Shemos 12:39)*

Q on the verse *Rashi* is bothered by a question. We understand that they were whisked out of Egypt so quickly that their dough did not have a chance to rise. So, why was it necessary to tell us "**nor had they made provisions for themselves**"?

A of the commentator He answers that the Torah is not just relating information—that they did not pack peanut butter and jelly sandwiches or snacks for the desert safari. Rather, it is praising the Jews for following G-d into the wilderness without any provisions.

Q on the commentator This *Rashi* is hard to comprehend. Had they forgotten the last ten months of miraculous plagues, witnessing G-d's wrath against the Egyptians while protecting and helping the Jewish nation? At the beginning of the plagues, it may have been difficult to leave without ample food supplies, but now it should be easy. And remember, they were oppressed for hundreds of years with extremely hard work and beatings, and, at times, their children were abducted and murdered. So, why the praise for doing something that should be so simple?

New insight We learn from this *Rashi* just how difficult it was for the Jews to leave with practically no food except the dough in their packs. Although they knew G-d had a free meal plan waiting, it was so hard to form this trust. That was why they were praised for pushing those feelings aside and placing their full faith in G-d.

Lesson for life As Jews, we have a special connection with G-d. We are His children, whom He loves dearly, and He is always taking care of all our needs. While it is difficult for us to feel this, the Torah is telling us that it was even a challenge for the generation who witnessed so many miracles. We must, however, know that it is possible to place our full faith in G-d, just like our ancestors did. *Chovos Halevavos* explains how we can achieve higher levels of faith in G-d by focusing on the things that have worked out for us over the course of our lives. While some levels of faith seem unattainable, the levels to which we can propel ourselves will provide an amazing amount of peace and tranquility. May we constantly grow in our faith in G-d and feel His abundant love and Providence.

BESHALACH

Crippling Fear

שמות יד:י: וּפַרְעֹה הִקְרִיב וַיִּשְׂאוּ בְנֵי יִשְׂרָאֵל אֶת עֵינֵיהֶם וְהִנֵּה
מִצְרַיִם נֹסֵעַ אַחֲרֵיהֶם וַיִּירְאוּ מְאֹד וַיִּצְעֲקוּ בְנֵי יִשְׂרָאֵל אֶל ה':

חזקוני: וייראו מאד מה ראו ישראל לירא כל כך משש מאות
רכב והלא הם היו ששים רבוא וכולם בני עשרים שנה ומעלה
וחלוצי צבא, כדכתיב וחמושים עלו בני ישראל, אלא יראים היו
להלחם עם אדוניהם, משל לעבד המפחד מאדוניו תמיד.

In *Parashas Beshalach*, the Jews find themselves pursued by the Egyptian army, seemingly cornered and trapped between the Egyptians on one side and the Red Sea on the other.

*Pharaoh approached; the Children of Israel raised their eyes and behold! Egypt was journeying after them, **and they were very frightened**…(Shemos 14:10)*

Q on the verse | The *Chizkuni* asks: The Jewish nation counted six hundred thousand armed men against six hundred Egyptians chariots. Why does the verse state, "**and they were very frightened**"? Frightened about what? I'll take those odds any day of the week!

A of the commentator | He answers that their fright was not a logical one; it was emotional in nature. The Jewish nation had intense angst about going up against their old masters and, accordingly, they were terrified. Anyone would have bet on the untrained six hundred thousand to beat the five thousand Egyptians, but they could not eradicate the slave mentality that had become ingrained in them for so many years.

Q on the commentator | This *Chizkuni* requires a closer look. Despite having been slaves for hundreds of years with all the emotional baggage that comes with it, they outnumbered the Egyptians 120 to one. It simply does not add up that they should be fearful of them in any significant way!

New insight | What he is teaching us is a deep insight into the human condition. If one has grown accustomed to being subservient and petrified of his master for decades, he can no longer break out of this mindset in such a short period of time. That is why they could not think straight when confronted by their masters.

Lesson for life | Fear can be a paralyzing feeling that causes us to shirk away from things that we could accomplish if it were not there. On the other hand, fear can be a healthy emotion that stops a child from running into ongoing traffic. We must be on guard to view every situation intellectually, never letting fear cripple us.

Who's Really Pulling
the Strings?

*Dedicated by Jane and Stanley Blum in memory
of their parents Marcia and George De Pinna
and Evelyn and Robert Blum*

שמות יד:טז: וְאַתָּה הָרֵם אֶת מַטְּךָ וּנְטֵה אֶת יָדְךָ עַל הַיָּם וּבְקָעֵהוּ
וְיָבֹאוּ בְנֵי יִשְׂרָאֵל בְּתוֹךְ הַיָּם בַּיַּבָּשָׁה:

פירוש הרא"ש: נטה את ידך על הים. שמעתי מפי אבא מרי ע"ה
שקריעת ים סוף לא נעשית במטה והטעם לפי שהיו מלעיבים
ומלעיגים על משה מלאך ה' צבאות והיו אומרים מה כוחו ומה
טיבו של משה והלא הקטן עמנו אלו היה מטה האלקים בידו
יעשה נסים ונפלאות כמוהו אז ראה והשקיף קל קנא יושב
בשמים וצוה למשה עבדו ואתה הרם את מטך פי' הפרישהו ממך
לשון תרומה ונטה את ידך על הים ובקעהו וכן עשה וזהו שאמר
הפסוק ויאמינו בה' ובמשה עבדו אז הרגישו היכולת שהיה ביד
משה בלתי מטה האלקים וחזרו והודו לראשונות.

In *Parashas Beshalach*, G-d instructs Moshe to split the sea
and free the Jewish nation from Egyptian slavery.

"And you—lift up your staff and stretch out your
arm over the sea and split it; and the Children of
Israel shall come into the midst of the sea on dry land."
(Shemos 14:16)

Q on the verse The *Rosh* (*Tur* and Rabbeinu Bachaya) is bothered by a question. Just a few verses later, the Torah says Moshe stretched out **his hand** and split the sea. What happened to his staff? (Maybe someone should check the lost and found!)

A of the commentator He answers that the Jewish People were saying, "Moshe can only do miracles with his staff. If you took it away and gave it to someone much less prestigious, he would also be able to perform all the same miracles." Therefore, G-d now instructs Moshe to show the world that he can split the sea even without his staff.

Q on the commentator The *Rosh's* commentary is puzzling. Moshe always proclaimed that he was merely a messenger of G-d and had no abilities of his own. Each time he warned of an impending plague, he foretold what G-d would do to the Egyptians if they did not let the Jewish nation go. Whenever the Egyptians begged for an affliction to be removed, Moshe announced that he would pray to G-d to remove it. It was not him; it was G-d! So why would the Jewish People be transfixed on Moshe's staff as if it was a magic wand?

New insight We learn from the *Rosh* an illuminating life lesson. People tend to be drawn to what they see. Time after time, the Jewish People saw Moshe and Aharon bringing plagues upon the Egyptians. As they witnessed the use of the staff each time, they started to forget Who was really pulling the strings. That is why Moshe was commanded to use his hand—to remind them Who was really in charge.

Lesson for life We often attribute success to our own hard work and become despondent when we encounter failure. Just as a puppeteer is really pulling the strings while hidden from view, so too G-d is running the show at all times and thus ensuring the very best outcome for us. At times, we see His Providence right away, and at other times we may not see it for weeks, months, or even years. Let us stop being mesmerized by "the Staff" and look beyond. Hashem is in control and helping at every juncture.

YISRO

Proper Etiquette

*Dedicated by Sal and Bonnie Hanono in memory
of Sal's parents Mordehai and Rahel Hanono*

שמות יח:ו: וַיֹּאמֶר אֶל מֹשֶׁה אֲנִי חֹתֶנְךָ יִתְרוֹ בָּא אֵלֶיךָ וְאִשְׁתְּךָ
וּשְׁנֵי בָנֶיהָ עִמָּהּ:

ספורנו: אני חותנך יתרו הקדים להודיעו דרך מוסר למען יוכל
להכין מקום לשבתם, כאמרם ז״ל (נדה פרק כל היד) אל תכנס
לביתך פתאום, כל שכן לבית חבירך.

In *Parashas Yisro*, the Torah tells us that after Moshe had been separated from his family for an extended period, his father-in-law, Yisro, brought them to rejoin Moshe. Yisro sends a message to Moshe that he is on his way and is bringing along his daughter, Tziporah, and her two sons.

> *He said to Moshe, "I, your father-in-law, Yisro, am coming to you, with your wife and her two sons with her." (Shemos 18:6)*

Q on the verse The *Sforno* is bothered by a question. If Yisro had not warned of their visit and just popped in, wouldn't Moshe have loved the surprise? Why the need to warn him in advance?

A of the commentator He answers that he had to give Moshe ample notice that they were on the way because it would be akin to "barging into someone's home without prior warning," which is not proper.

Q on the commentator This *Sforno* is hard to understand. Everyone knows that it is improper to intrude on your neighbor suddenly because they will not be prepared to have you. But this is surely different. After such a long separation, Moshe would be ecstatic to see his family, so there is practically no downside. They were surely not running out of tent space in the desert, and the manna fell from heaven, bringing them daily sustenance. So, what is the issue here?

New insight We learn from this *Sforno* just how nuanced proper etiquette can be. Even though Moshe would have been thrilled at the surprise, it is simply not polite to show up without warning, family or not. Yisro understood this and courteously sent him a message in advance.

Lesson for life Let us always try to be a *mensch* in every given situation, taking into account the other person's needs and sensitivities. May we become greater people who constantly show care and concern for others.

Gratitude:
The Great Motivator

---

*Dedicated by Sal and Bonnie Hanono in memory of
Bonnie's grandparents Robert and Esther Medwed*

שמות יח:ז: וַיֵּצֵא מֹשֶׁה לִקְרַאת חֹתְנוֹ וַיִּשְׁתַּחוּ וַיִּשַּׁק לוֹ וַיִּשְׁאֲלוּ אִישׁ
לְרֵעֵהוּ לְשָׁלוֹם וַיָּבֹאוּ הָאֹהֱלָה:

ספורנו: ויצא משה לא חדל בשביל מעלתו לקדם פני מי ששלם
לו טובה בעת צר לו...

Parashas *Yisro* describes the reunion between Moshe and
his father-in-law, Yisro, in the desert.

*Moshe **went out to welcome his father-in-law**,
and he prostrated himself and kissed him, and each
inquired about the other's well-being; then they came
to the tent. (Shemos 18:7)*

_{Q on the verse}
The *Sforno* is bothered by a question: Why does the verse need
to tell us that Moshe "**went out to welcome his father-in-law**"?
Wouldn't we assume Moshe would act with common decency?

83

A of the
commentator He answers that, on a slight level, Moshe felt it was beneath him to interrupt whatever he was involved in to greet Yisro now. Moshe pushed through that feeling, however, and acted immediately by focusing on the memory that Yisro had helped him during his time of need.

Q on the
commentator This *Sforno* is difficult to understand. Why did Moshe need to concentrate on the fact that Yisro had previously helped him? If the proper action was to greet Yisro promptly and personally, shouldn't Moshe do that regardless of feeling gratitude or repaying an act of kindness?

New
insight This *Sforno* is teaching us that harnessing the power of *hakaras hatov* (gratitude) is an extremely powerful tool to motivate us to do what is right. Moshe understood this truth and utilized this strategy to act quickly and enthusiastically.

Lesson
for life We often know rationally how we should act in a situation, but emotions can cloud our judgment. As they say, "The heart and mind can be miles apart." Focusing on *hakaras hatov* is an effective way to overcome our reluctant feelings and do the right thing. By recalling the countless acts of kindness our parents, friends, and teachers have done for us, we can reciprocate with genuine eagerness and alacrity.

MISHPATIM

The Power
of Imagination

Dedicated by Leene and Bob Chavez to their parents
Gertrude and Hy Chase and Esther and Tom Thorney

שמות כב:כד: אִם כֶּסֶף תַּלְוֶה אֶת עַמִּי אֶת הֶעָנִי עִמָּךְ לֹא תִהְיֶה
לוֹ כְּנֹשֶׁה לֹא תְשִׂימוּן עָלָיו נֶשֶׁךְ:

רש"י: אֶת הֶעָנִי עִמָּךְ. הֱוֵי מִסְתַּכֵּל בְּעַצְמְךָ כְּאִלּוּ אַתָּה עָנִי.

Parashas *Mishpatim* delves into many interpersonal commandments, including proper dealings with money.

You should lend money to My people, to the poor person
who is with you; *do not act towards him as a creditor;*
do not lay interest upon him. (Shemos 22:24)

Q on the
verse

Rashi is bothered by a question. Why doesn't the verse just tell
us to lend to the poor person and not charge him interest? What
is the meaning behind the words, **"who is with you"**?

A of the commentator He answers that the words **"who is with you"** are teaching that we are commanded to picture ourselves "as if" we are with the destitute person in his situation when making the loan and therefore will not desire to charge him interest.

Q on the commentator This *Rashi* sounds like a wonderful idea to help us be sensitive to the poor man's plight, but how is it based in reality? The poor man is sleeping in the streets with no heat, no running water, and no food, while we have all these luxuries. Can we really feel what it is like to be in his shoes?

New insight *Rashi* is teaching us an important lesson. The power of imagination is so strong and vital to how we properly take care of others who are less fortunate. The Torah could have told us that we are simply obligated to do *chessed* (kindness) with those who are in need. Instead, it informs us that if we only make the effort, we have the potential to tap into a wellspring of sensitivity toward others.

Lesson for life We often take for granted our incredible imagination, assuming that it was created just to enjoy books, shows, or generate new ideas for practical or artistic purposes. However, G-d gave us this special gift to hone our senses not only for these endeavors but to empathize deeply with our fellow man. In this way, we can greatly improve our character and profoundly help others with a level of compassion we never knew was possible.

Jewish Meditation

*Dedicated by Leene and Bob Chavez to their parents
Gertrude and Hy Chase and Esther and Tom Thorney*

שמות כב:כז: אֱלֹהִים לֹא תְקַלֵּל וְנָשִׂיא בְעַמְּךָ לֹא תָאֹר:

ספורנו: אלהים לא תקלל אף על פי שתחשוב שהטה את דינך
הדיין לא תקללהו, שאין אדם רואה חובה לעצמו.

In *Parashas Mishpatim*, the Torah speaks about someone who
had a conflict with others and got upset that the outcome
did not go his way.

> **You shall not revile a judge**, and you shall not curse
> a leader among our people. (Shemos 22:27)

The *Sforno* tells us that even if you think that the judge skewed
the judgment against you, do not curse him. Why? Because
a person never sees clearly when he's in the wrong.

This *Sforno* seems to be saying something very basic and ele-
mentary. Of course, people often do not see clearly when they

87

have been ruled against and think they are in the right! So, what new insight is he teaching us?

New insight We learn from this *Sforno* a profound lesson. When the angry litigant reads this in the Torah, it is possible for him to totally change his outlook. This is done by *mussar b'hispaalus* (practical *mussar*). If he sits in a quiet moment of meditation and self-introspection, assessing everything with an open mind, he can reset his way of thinking and reframe the way he sees the situation. This will allow him to not only stymie his frustration but even acknowledge that he was wrong.

Lesson for life The great *mussar* (personal growth) thinkers spoke about this concept in great detail: the great difficulty in changing a character trait and the need for deep, meaningful contemplation and self-critique in order to grow. This is one of the best ways to break free from our perception of reality and see another person's point of view. May we merit to see the world clearly, always growing and improving ourselves.

TERUMAH

Untapped Potential

Dedicated by Howard Ain in memory
of his late wife Susan

שמות כה:ט: כְּכֹל אֲשֶׁר אֲנִי מַרְאֶה אוֹתְךָ אֵת תַּבְנִית הַמִּשְׁכָּן וְאֵת
תַּבְנִית כָּל כֵּלָיו וְכֵן תַּעֲשׂוּ:

רמב"ן: וכן תעשו—ועל דרך הפשט אין צורך לכל זה, אבל בא
הכפל לחזוק וזרוז.

Parashas Terumah speaks about the construction of the
holy Tabernacle and its vessels.

They shall make a Sanctuary for Me—so that I may
dwell among them. Like everything that I show you,
the form of the Tabernacle and the form of all its ves-
sels; and so shall you do. (Shemos 25:9)

Q on the verse

Ramban is bothered by the seemingly redundant words, "**and so**
shall you do." What new information do we learn?

A of the commentator

He answers that these words are used to encourage alacrity
while building and constructing all the vessels of the Tabernacle.

89

Q on the
commentator This *Ramban* is hard to understand. The Jewish People were working on the most important project in history: G-d's home on earth! The Tabernacle was the conduit for forgiveness and unparalleled spiritual connection to the Creator. It would host the showbreads that miraculously stayed warm and fresh for an entire week, an eternal flame that was always lit, and so much more. Wouldn't the craftsman give it their utmost?

New
insight We learn from this *Ramban* a key to understanding motivation. We may be eager to accomplish, yet when we think we have hit our limit, we can tap into powerful inner reserves that propel us higher than we ever thought possible. G-d therefore instructed Moshe to utilize this tool to drive the craftsmen to produce at a level they never realized was feasible.

Lesson
for life Each and every day, we try to utilize our G-d-given talents to accomplish. Whether it be a project, a job, or a difficulty, it may be very hard. On the flip side, we may be enthused by something we love and know to be vital, but even so, at a certain point we hit a wall with no gas left in the tank. "There's only so much I can do," we tell ourselves. The amazing take-home here is that that is incorrect. We may need a break, but with alacrity and excitement, we can make the improbable happen and the impossible possible.

Looking beneath
the Surface

*Dedicated by Howard Ain in memory
of his parents Helen and David Ain*

שמות כה:י–יא: וְעָשׂוּ אֲרוֹן עֲצֵי שִׁטִּים אַמָּתַיִם וָחֵצִי אָרְכּוֹ וְאַמָּה
וָחֵצִי רָחְבּוֹ וְאַמָּה וָחֵצִי קֹמָתוֹ: וְצִפִּיתָ אֹתוֹ זָהָב טָהוֹר מִבַּיִת וּמִחוּץ
תְּצַפֶּנּוּ וְעָשִׂיתָ עָלָיו זֵר זָהָב סָבִיב:

רש״י: מבית ומחוץ תצפנו. נָתַן שֶׁל עֵץ בְּתוֹךְ שֶׁל זָהָב וְשֶׁל זָהָב
בְּתוֹךְ שֶׁל עֵץ וְחִפָּה שְׂפָתוֹ הָעֶלְיוֹנָה בְּזָהָב, נִמְצָא מְצוּפֶּה מִבַּיִת
וּמִחוּץ. (יומא ע״ב)

שפתי חכמים: בתנחומא (ויקהל ז) נתן טעם שמרמז כשם שהארון
אף על פי שהעץ נתן בתוכו אתה נוהג בו כבוד, כך אתה רואה
בני תורה שהמה עניים נהוג בם כבוד בשביל תורתם.

P arashas Terumah describes how the holy vessels in the
Tabernacle were to be constructed.

You shall make an Ark of acacia wood, two-and-
a-half cubits its length; a cubit-and-a-half its width;

91

and a cubit-and-a-half its height. You shall cover it with pure gold, from within and from without shall you cover it, and you shall make on it a gold crown all around." (Shemos 25:10–11)

Rashi (with *Sifsei Chachamim*) tells us that the beautiful Ark was encased in gold both on the inside and outside. If so, they ask, why did G-d instruct, "**you shall make an Ark of acacia wood**" to be sandwiched between the layers of gold? Why should less precious material be used for the Ark?

Sifsei Chachamim brings the *Tanchuma*, which says that G-d is teaching a lesson by means of a metaphor. Often, poor Torah scholars are not accorded proper respect. Instead of a holy person, people see only the exterior: a lowly pauper. Therefore, G-d says, "Place a lower-quality material in my vessel and focus on its value and purpose, and so too with a devoted Jew, look beyond his exterior and honor him, because he imbibes himself with spirituality and Torah."

This is hard to do. We all know that the person dressed in dignified clothing will gain more respect from the masses than a poor person in shabby garbs, regardless of their inner virtues. Such is a reality of life. Could looking at the Ark really have an impact on people?

We learn from this *Rashi* an astounding lesson. The same individual who judges the poor person based on his appearance can pivot 180-degrees and change. Observing G-d's Ark and realizing that this vessel used for the most exalted purpose was made from material of inferior quality is a powerful lesson. Understanding this profound message from G-d can leave an imprint on a person and how he perceives others.

When we judge others superficially, our perception is heavily skewed. We form opinions based on what we can see when the true value of a person exists below the surface. We know that after 120 years when we enter the World of Truth, we will see people for who they truly are. Exalted souls who were "nobodies" in this world based on society's standards will be sitting high on a pedestal. Let us strive to see the G-dliness in those we meet and accord them the respect they deserve, both in this world and the next!

TETZAVEH

Where Is Moshe?

Dedicated by
Rabbi and Mrs. Avrohom and Rena Richmond
in memory of their grandmother
Esther Shayndel bas Baruch Bendett

בעל הטורים שמות כז:כ: ואתה תצוה לא הזכיר משה בזה הסדר
משא״כ בכל החומש שמשעה שנולד משה אין סדר שלא הוזכר
בה...ועוד דזו הפרשה מדברת בטכסיסי כהונה. וממשה היתה
הכהונה הגדולה לצאת, אלא על ידי שסרב לילך בשליחות
המקום, נטלה ממנו ונתנה לאהרן. לכן לא נזכר שמו של משה
בפרשה זו מפני עגמת נפשו.

שמות ד:יד: וַיִּחַר אַף ה׳ בְּמֹשֶׁה וַיֹּאמֶר הֲלֹא אַהֲרֹן אָחִיךָ הַלֵּוִי
יָדַעְתִּי כִּי דַבֵּר יְדַבֵּר הוּא וְגַם הִנֵּה הוּא יֹצֵא לִקְרָאתֶךָ וְרָאֲךָ וְשָׂמַח
בְּלִבּוֹ:

רש״י: הלא אהרן אחיך הלוי: שהיה עתיד להיות לוי ולא כהן,
והכהונה הייתי אומר לצאת ממך, מעתה לא יהיה כן אלא הוא
יהיה כהן ואתה לוי...

צדה לדרך: ולכן אחר שסירב משה כולי האי כל שבעת ימים
בשביל כבוד אחיו, אמר לו הקדוש ברוך הוא אתה יותר חס על

94

כבוד אחיך ממה שאתה חס על כבודי שהרי אין מסרבין לגדול
כדפירוש רשי לעיל בפסוק ויאמרו לא כי ברחוב נלין וגוי הלכך
אין אתה ראוי לכהונה.

Parashas *Tetzaveh* has no mention of Moshe for the first time since he was born. He appears in every *parashah* in four of the five books of the Torah with only this exception.

The *Baal Haturim* explains that Moshe had attempted to defer the mission of freeing the Jewish People to his older brother when G-d appeared to him in the burning bush. Because of this, he lost out on his family becoming the Kohanim, and they instead remained simple Levites. Hashem knew that it would be hurtful to list Moshe in this *parashah* that speaks all about the Kohanim and their holy garments.

The Torah records Moshe's refusal to G-d at the burning bush:

> The wrath of Hashem burned against Moshe, and He said, "Is there not **Aharon your brother, the Levite**? I know that he will surely speak; moreover, behold, he is going out to meet you, and when he sees you, he will rejoice in his heart." (Shemos 4:14)

Q on the verse

Rashi (with *Sifsei Chachamim*) is bothered by a question. Why does the Torah refer to "**Aharon, your brother, the Levite**," when we know that he became a Kohen?

A of the commentator

He answers that Aharon should have been the Levite; however, from this point forward, Moshe became the Levite and Aharon the Kohen as a result of Moshe's attempt to refuse G-d's directive to lead the Jews from Egypt.

Q on the commentator

Tzeidah Laderech asks, what did Moshe do wrong? He was not being lazy. Rather, he was proposing to G-d that his older brother, Aharon, who had been the Jewish leader and prophet for decades, should take this position. Isn't that wonderful that he was displaying humility and honoring his older brother instead of grabbing this opportunity for himself?

He answers that *Rashi* is teaching us that although Moshe had the very best intentions of honoring his brother, he made a miscalculation that caused him to dishonor Hashem on some level. Of course, he wanted to show the utmost respect to Hashem, but he focused too much on Aharon's honor, thereby causing him to inadvertently make Hashem's honor secondary. Because of that, he lost the right to the *kehunah* and also earned a lesser position as a Levite.

Lesson for life Remember the days of cramming for a big test? Imagine we studied and studied and stayed up all night, but then forgot to go to class to take the exam, resulting in a zero. Sometimes we get so caught up in an important project that we lose sight of the big picture. If it can happen to Moshe, it can definitely happen to us. Let us take this lesson to heart by always reassessing what we are doing and why we are doing it. Then, we will arrive at the right decisions followed by the correct actions in all we do.

Dressing Appropriately

Dedicated by
Rabbi and Mrs. Avrohom and Rena Richmond in memory
of their grandfather Chaim Yosef Tzvi ben Henach

שמות כח:ה: וְהֵם יִקְחוּ אֶת הַזָּהָב וְאֶת הַתְּכֵלֶת וְאֶת הָאַרְגָּמָן וְאֶת
תּוֹלַעַת הַשָּׁנִי וְאֶת הַשֵּׁשׁ:

חזקוני: והם החכמי לב יקחו את הזהב המבואר במקום אחר
הוא זהב התרומה המפורש בפרשת תרומה, שכשם שאני רוצה
שיקחו את התרומה לצורך המשכן כן אני רוצה שיקחו את הזהב
ואת התרומה לבגדים ולא יאמרו אהרן מבקש לעצמו, שהרי
בגדים מכפרים על ישראל כדאמרינן לקמן.

Parashas *Tetzaveh* speaks about the Kohanim's holy garments, the materials from which they were made, and
their purpose.

> ***They shall take*** *the gold, the turquoise, purple, and*
> *scarlet wool, and the linen. (Shemos 28:5)*

Chizkuni is bothered by a question. **Who** should take the gold
and other materials and for **whom**?

A of the commentator He answers that **the craftsmen** should take the same materials that were previously donated for the Tabernacle and use them in making Aharon's garments. Hashem was saying, "Just as I wanted these items donated for My Tabernacle, here too, I would like these materials used by the holy Kohanim for their garments. And the people should not say, "Aharon wants this for himself. Rather, he should wear these garments to assist him in getting forgiveness for the Jewish nation."

Q on the commentator This *Chizkuni* is difficult to comprehend. Does G-d really need to tell the people that the righteous Aharon would never desire the gold for himself and only has pure intentions in mind while wearing the holy garments in the Tabernacle?

New insight We learn from this *Chizkuni* an amazing lesson. Of course, Aharon would never illegally take the materials, and he would only have the best intentions while wearing these garments. Furthermore, he performed the service on behalf of the people to get forgiveness on Yom Kippur. However, when wearing the beautiful, intricately designed, and expensive garments, it was still possible for the wearer to be affected by them on some level and not concentrate completely on being the emissary of the people. Even Aharon the High Priest could have a slight level of ego creep in while wearing these royal priestly vestments.

Lesson for life It is so important to dress nicely and in an honorable and respectful manner. However, we must be vigilant when getting ready to go out in our finest not to let our good looks make us feel too haughty. Let us always realize that we are dignified and created in the image of G-d and yet carry ourselves with a sense of humility.

KI SISA

Just Add a Smile

Dedicated by Warren and Nancy Factor
in honor of friends, family and Jews who helped
and prayed for refuah for our son Ely David Factor.
May he continue to have good health, success,
and mazel with Hashem's help.

שמות לב:יט: וַיְהִי כַּאֲשֶׁר קָרַב אֶל הַמַּחֲנֶה וַיַּרְא אֶת הָעֵגֶל וּמְחֹלֹת וַיִּחַר אַף מֹשֶׁה וַיַּשְׁלֵךְ מִידוֹ [מִיָּדָיו] אֶת הַלֻּחֹת וַיְשַׁבֵּר אֹתָם תַּחַת הָהָר:

ספורנו: וירא את העגל ומחולות ויחר אף משה כשראה שהיו שמחים בקלקול שעשו, כענין כי רעת כי אז תעלוזי ובזה התקצף ונואש שיוכל לתקן המעוות באופן שיחזרו לתמותם ויהיו ראוים לאותן הלוחות.

I n *Parashas Ki Sisa*, after forty days and forty nights on Mt. Sinai, Moshe returns. He intended to give the Tablets to the Jewish People, but these plans end up changing rather quickly:

> It happened, as he drew near the camp and saw the calf and **the dances**, that Moshe's anger flared up. He

99

> *threw down the Tablets from his hands and shattered*
> *them at the foot of the mountain. (Shemos 32:19)*

Q on the verse *Sforno* is bothered by a question. The Jewish People had mistakenly miscounted the arrival date of Moshe and began worshipping the golden calf as his replacement. As Moshe approaches and they realize their mistake, shouldn't he assume that they will now deeply regret their actions, recognize their mistake, and return to their previous spiritual state? Why then did he proceed to break the Tablets?

A of the commentator He answers that when Moshe saw "**the dances**" with joy, he felt the situation was now hopeless. The exuberance they expressed while transgressing this sin caused him to feel that they were no longer deserving of these Tablets, and he proceeded to smash them.

Q on the commentator This *Sforno* is puzzling. Moshe was a tremendous leader who loved the Jewish People dearly and never gave up on them. What about the fact that they worshiped an idol and committed a slew of other sins? Did those things not bother Moshe? Why did he choose to single out the dancing with joy?

New insight We learn from this *Sforno* a profound lesson. A person could go as far as committing one of the three Jewish cardinal sins, and still come back from it. The situation is entirely different, however, when one is involved in these sins while simultaneously dancing around with pure *simchah* (joy). Such behavior takes things to a whole new level. The tireless and devoted leader, Moshe, realized that one can never totally come back from that.

Lesson for life Every single day of our lives, we have opportunities to do mitzvos and *aveiros* (sins). At times, we do the right thing, and at times, we do not; we are human. However, we must perceive that when we add *simchah* to the equation, it brings our actions to a whole new level. If we do give in to our evil inclination, we should always remember that, though we may have failed this time, we should not be happy about it. A little Jewish guilt is good! May we merit to not only do more and more mitzvos, but to upgrade them in quality with a smile on our faces.

Cognitive Dissonance

Dedicated by Warren and Nancy Factor
in honor of friends, family and Jews who helped
and prayed for refuah for our son Ely David Factor.
May he continue to have good health, success,
and mazel with Hashem's help.

שמות לד:כט: וַיְהִי בְּרֶדֶת מֹשֶׁה מֵהַר סִינַי וּשְׁנֵי לֻחֹת הָעֵדֻת בְּיַד
מֹשֶׁה בְּרִדְתּוֹ מִן הָהָר וּמֹשֶׁה לֹא יָדַע כִּי קָרַן עוֹר פָּנָיו בְּדַבְּרוֹ אִתּוֹ:

חזקוני: לפי שרצו להעמיד להם מנהיג במקום משה הראה להם
הקב"ה שהוא מלא מזיו שכינתו על פיו ואין להעמיד אחר במקומו.

דעת זקנים: והנה קרן. ולפי שטעו ורצו להעמיד מנהיג במקומו
האיר הקב"ה אותו מזיו שכינתו להראות להן שלא היה מנהיג
ראוי כמוהו.

At the end of the *Parashas Ki Sisa*, Moshe returns to the Jewish People as their rightful leader bringing the second set of Tablets, and G-d blesses him with a rare present.

When Moshe descended from Mount Sinai—with the two Tablets of Testimony in the hand of Moshe as he

102

*descended from the mountain—Moshe did not know that **the skin of his face had become radiant** when He had spoken to him. (Shemos 34:29)*

Q on the verse *Chizkuni* and *Daas Zekeinim* want to know why G-d felt it necessary to make **"the skin of his face radiant."**

A of the commentator They answer that the nation had replaced Moshe with the golden calf previously, which resulted in him breaking the Tablets and ascending to heaven to get the second set. G-d felt a need to show the Jewish People that Moshe was such an extraordinary leader that He made "the skin of his face radiant." Now, without a doubt, they would reinstate him to his rightful position.

Q on the commentator *Chizkuni* and *Daas Zekeinim* are hard to comprehend. The people knew that they made an enormous mistake by worshipping the golden calf and making it Moshe's replacement. They repented, apologized, and begged Moshe to seek forgiveness from G-d and return with a new set of Tablets. Wouldn't they welcome him back with open arms (without any need for a miracle), showing he was special beyond any other potential leader?

New insight We learn from this *Chizkuni* and *Daas Zekeinim* that, although they knew they had erred in replacing Moshe, they were experiencing cognitive dissonance. This blocked them from seeing the reality that he was the most qualified on many levels for this position. A part of their subconscious still felt that there was a justifiable reason for "letting him go," even though they knew rationally that this was wrong and were remorseful for their sin. G-d knew this and endowed Moshe with a superhuman countenance, as if to say, "He is so uniquely qualified, do not even think of replacing him."

Lesson for life When we make a decision or commit to a plan that ends up failing, we have a hard time believing that we made a mistake. It is natural to want to defend our opinions and decisions, but convincing ourselves that we are infallible can harm us in major ways. Let us have an open mind and be receptive to new information so that we may truly grow and succeed.

Because I Said So

Dedicated on behalf of Daniel, Jeffrey,
and Robert Abramson in memory of their loving
wife and mother Jane Abramson

שמות לה:ל: וַיֹּאמֶר מֹשֶׁה אֶל בְּנֵי יִשְׂרָאֵל רְאוּ קָרָא ה׳ בְּשֵׁם
בְּצַלְאֵל בֶּן אוּרִי בֶן חוּר לְמַטֵּה יְהוּדָה:

דעת זקנים: מהו ראו לפי שכשאמר משה לישראל שבצלאל
יעשה המשכן היו ישראל מרננים אחרי משה ואומרים שכל
הגדולה הוא נוטל לו ולמשפחתו אמר להם משה דעו וראו כי
לא מדעתי אני עושה אלא מפי הקב״ה ואף משה עצמו בשעה
שאמר לו הקב״ה על מלאכת המשכן ועשית היה סבור לעשות
הכל אמר לו הקב״ה לא כאשר עולה בדעתך אלא צדיק שנהרג
על מעשה העגל דהיינו חור יבא בן בנו ויעשנו לפי שהמשכן
כפרה על אותו מעשה וזהו שאמר לו הקב״ה ראה קראתי.

In *Parashas Vayakhel*, the craftsmen are selected for the special job of making the vessels for the Tabernacle.

*Moshe said to the Children of Israel, "**See**, Hashem has proclaimed by name, Betzalel, son of Uri son of Chur, of the tribe of Yehudah. (Shemos 35:30)*

Q on the verse

Daas Zekeinim is bothered by why the Torah uses the extra word "**see**." Why not just say the verse without it? What does it add?

A of the commentator

He answers that the people were, once again, complaining to Moshe about nepotism, since he entrusted the head-craftsman job to his nephew, Betzalel. Therefore, he clarified his actions in great detail: "I initially assumed that I would be entrusted with this job, but G-d informed me otherwise. For the Tabernacle to bring atonement for the sin of the golden calf, G-d said we need someone who descends from a person who died trying to stop that sin. Only then will we be forgiven. That's why G-d picked a grandson of Chur, who was lynched trying to do the right thing during that episode."

Q on the commentator

This *Daas Zekeinim* is hard to understand. Why didn't Moshe just tell the Jewish People he was simply following orders from G-d and that Betzalel was best suited for this position? Why the whole megillah? He was Moshe, the greatest leader to ever live, who was known as the ultimate *eved Hashem* (servant of G-d). Shouldn't that be enough without any need for him to expound further?

New insight

We learn from this *Daas Zekeinim* an important life lesson. You can have someone as humble, dedicated, and honest as Moshe, and yet, when a negative thought pops into the heads of those around him, he needs to take the time not just to defend himself but to give explanation in a way that they will comprehend. In this manner, they will fully digest what he has to say and feel better about it.

Lesson for life

So many times, we have the feeling that we do not need to explain ourselves to others who may have jumped to the wrong conclusion. If we want to not only be in the clear but to achieve full cooperation from those around us, it is essential to share the reasoning behind our actions whenever possible. Whether it be friends, family, co-workers, or siblings, we learn from this example that it is of the utmost importance to take the time and make the effort to explain why we acted the way we did.

True Leadership

*Dedicated on behalf of Daniel, Jeffrey,
and Robert Abramson in memory of their loving
wife and mother Jane Abramson*

שמות לט:מג: וַיַּרְא מֹשֶׁה אֶת כָּל הַמְּלָאכָה וְהִנֵּה עָשׂוּ אֹתָהּ כַּאֲשֶׁר
צִוָּה ה' כֵּן עָשׂוּ וַיְבָרֶךְ אֹתָם מֹשֶׁה:

רלב״ג: וירא משה את כל המלאכה והנה עשו אותה כאשר צוה
ה' כן עשו ויברך אותם משה. למדנו מזה שראוי למנהיג הדור
לברך המונהגי׳ ממנו כאשר ישמעו אל דבריו כדי שיהיו יותר
זריזים לעשות רצונו.

In *Parashas Pekudei*, the craftsmen finish the job of making all
the vessels for the Tabernacle.

> *Moshe saw the entire work, and behold!—they had
> done it as Hashem had commanded, so they had done!*
> ***And Moshe blessed them.*** *(Shemos 39:43)*

Q on the verse *Ralbag* questions why the verse ends with "**and Moshe blessed
them.**" Surely, the craftsmen were told that they did a great job,
so why the need to bless them here?

107

A of the
commentator He answers that if one wants his team to feel great about their accomplishments and have alacrity when working on future projects, he must make a special effort to bless them. This is what the Torah was highlighting here!

Q on the
commentator This *Ralbag* is puzzling. Moshe was a gifted leader who knew all the books on proper management. One can assume that he was always positive with his people by complimenting them often and urging them onward. In addition, the craftsmen were enthused to be handpicked as the team that would "build G-d's home." "Do what you love, and you will never work a day in your life" was in their hearts and minds as they immersed themselves in this mission. So why the necessity for the extra blessing and encouragement here?

New
insight We learn from this *Ralbag* the invaluable lesson of how far one needs to go to bring out the best in others. Even with his constant positive feedback and encouragement, Moshe knew the craftsmen would feel even better about themselves and their projects if blessed and inspired yet again.

Lesson
for life I recently asked the CEO of a bank how he motivated so many in his company to work literally around the clock, including Sundays and many late nights, until a very important project was completed. He shared that he met with all his staff to explain the vital importance of processing and submitting the PPP grants for the nonprofits. Not only would they directly help those organizations, but they would allow countless people who are employed by the nonprofits to retain their jobs, provide for their families, and put food on the table. He coupled this with constant compliments, encouragement, and blessings, and this particular bank was rewarded with success on a level previously unseen. We are all leaders to those in our sphere of influence. Let us take Moshe's lesson to heart, making a difference to those around us and in the broader community.

Sefer Vayikra

Dedicated by
Craig Beresin
in honor of my parents
Marc and Phyllis Beresin
and all the Rabbis, like Rabbi Shimon Feder,
who do such a great job teaching Torah!

VAYIKRA

Does Power Corrupt?

*Dedicated in honor of our son Yaakov David HaKohen,
who makes us proud and gives us nachas with his path
of Torah, fine middos, and his striving love
and connection to Hashem. We love you.
From Mommy and Aba, Susie and Alan Berger*

ויקרא ד:כב–כג: אֲשֶׁר נָשִׂיא יֶחֱטָא וְעָשָׂה אַחַת מִכָּל מִצְוֹת ה'
אֱלֹקָיו אֲשֶׁר לֹא תֵעָשֶׂינָה בִּשְׁגָגָה וְאָשֵׁם: אוֹ הוֹדַע אֵלָיו חַטָּאתוֹ
אֲשֶׁר חָטָא בָּהּ וְהֵבִיא אֶת קָרְבָּנוֹ שְׂעִיר עִזִּים זָכָר תָּמִים:

ספורנו: כִּי אָמְנָם זֶה דָּבָר מָצוּי שֶׁיֶּחֱטָא, כְּאָמְרוֹ "וַיִּשְׁמַן יְשֻׁרוּן
וַיִּבְעָט". (דברים לב, טו)

Parashas *Vayikra* explains what happens when a Jewish ruler sins.

When a ruler sins, and commits one from among all the commandments of Hashem, his G-d, that may not be done—unintentionally—and becomes guilty. If the sin that he committed becomes known to him, he shall bring his offering...(Vayikra 4:22–23)

111

Q on the verse *Sforno* is bothered by the wording "**when a ruler sins**," because it implies that it is inevitable that a ruler will sin. Who says he will sin, especially with regards to a *nasi*? The *nesi'im* were the greatest rabbis who possessed the highest caliber of Torah wisdom and *mussar* (character refinement).

A of the commentator He answers that people in positions of power are likely to sin, as the Torah says, "And they became fat and kicked" against G-d, having indulged in their wealth and power, which caused them to go astray. Sinning is not a matter of "if" but "when!"

Q on the commentator The *Sforno* is perplexing. If these people are truly righteous and achieved their positions because of their outstanding qualities, how can he say that they will let their prominence get to their heads and that they are likely to sin?

New insight We learn from the *Sforno* about the dangers that can accompany the acquisition of power. When the "cream of the crop"—the absolute best of society—rise to power, their newfound positions can corrupt who they are and what they stand for. Therefore, they must always be extremely vigilant as to where they have gone astray and what they can to do to rectify things.

Lesson for life It is famously said that, "Power corrupts and absolute power corrupts absolutely." The Torah does not believe that people are inherently bad, nor that power makes people evil. The greatest of Jewish men came to their positions because they were people of the highest caliber deserving of such an honor. Nonetheless, power makes people—all people—somewhat more susceptible to transgressions. Whether we achieve the position of *nasi* or CEO, we must always be careful not to let power and prominence lead us down the wrong path.

Hashem Loves Us

ויקרא ד:כד: וְסָמַךְ יָדוֹ עַל רֹאשׁ הַשָּׂעִיר וְשָׁחַט אֹתוֹ בִּמְקוֹם אֲשֶׁר
יִשְׁחַט אֶת הָעֹלָה לִפְנֵי ה' חַטָּאת הוּא:

חזקוני: במקום אשר ישחט את העלה שלא לבייש מי שחטא
ויהיו הרואים סבורים שהיא עולה.

A verse from *Parashas Vayikra* says:

> *He shall lean his hand on the head of the goat, and he*
> *shall slaughter it in the place he would slaughter the*
> *elevation-offering before Hashem; it is a sin-offering.*
> *(Vayikra 4:24)*

There is more to this verse than meets the eye.

113

The
commentator
explains
The *Chizkuni* says that the reason why Hashem is instructing him to bring his sin offering in the same place as the elevation-offering is so that a bystander will not embarrass him by seeing that he's bringing a sin-offering. A bystander will reason, "Who says he did a sin? Maybe he's bringing an elevation-offering." The *Chizkuni* further elaborates that in Hashem's original plan, each offering initially had a separate, designated place, and yet the location of the offering was changed for the aforementioned reason.

Q on the
commentator
This *Chizkuni* is difficult to understand for the following reasons:

1. People were not hanging around the Temple idly. It is unlikely that several people would see this. If you were there, you were there to fulfill a purpose and would most likely be busy with that.
2. Bringing a sin-offering was only allowed when the mistake was done by accident and you were seeking forgiveness. Even if someone noticed, it was not likely to be an embarrassment for the person bringing it. In fact, it showed that the person cared to rectify even the smallest transgressions.
3. Hashem, the Architect of the World, had a clear plan set for where each thing should go. Yet, we learn He changed His plans. Why?

New
insight
Here lies an amazing lesson learned from this *Chizkuni*. Even when almost no one would notice someone bringing a sin-offering, and it would be of minimal embarrassment, it is still worth Hashem altering his design plans in His home on Earth to spare even the possibility of one of His children feeling shame.

Lesson
for life
Recently, the world experienced a very difficult and confusing situation. We may have wondered why G-d did not want us going to work, school, and to synagogues. What was He thinking? Had He forgotten about us? Rest assured, Hashem cares for us more than we could ever imagine, and He is orchestrating the world—and every minuscule detail and nuance of it—for our ultimate benefit.

TZAV

Above Suspicion

Dedication of this parashah is by the Zemmel Family

וַיִּקְרָא ח:ה: וַיֹּאמֶר מֹשֶׁה אֶל הָעֵדָה זֶה הַדָּבָר אֲשֶׁר צִוָּה ה' לַעֲשׂוֹת:

רש"י: זֶה הַדָּבָר. דְּבָרִים שֶׁתִּרְאוּ שֶׁאֲנִי עוֹשֶׂה לִפְנֵיכֶם, צִוַּנִי הַקָּבָּ"ה לַעֲשׂוֹת, וְאַל תֹּאמְרוּ לִכְבוֹדִי וְלִכְבוֹד אָחִי אֲנִי עוֹשֶׂה.

שפתי חכמים: וְאַף עַל פִּי שֶׁמֹּשֶׁה הָיָה יוֹדֵעַ שֶׁסּוֹף הַכָּבוֹד לָבֹא וְשֶׁתִּשְׁרֶה הַשְּׁכִינָה בְּקָרְבְּנוֹתָיו וּמִמֵּילָא יָדְעוּ שֶׁכָּל זֶה הָיָה מְצֻוֶּה הַשֵּׁם יִתְבָּרַךְ, אֲפִילוּ הָכִי הָיָה רוֹצֶה לְהוֹצִיא עַצְמוֹ מִן הַחֲשָׁד אֲפִילוּ רֶגַע אֶחָד.

Parashas Tzav speaks about Moshe helping his brother Aharon and Aharon's sons as he prepares them to serve in the Holy Tabernacle.

Moshe said to the assembly, **"This is the thing that Hashem commanded to be done."** *Moshe brought Aharon and his sons forward and he immersed them in water. He placed the Tunic upon him...(Vayikra 8:5–7)*

Q on the verse   *Rashi* questions why Moshe had to specifically point out to everyone, **"This is the thing that Hashem commanded to be done."** Wasn't he always carrying out G-d's directives?

A of the commentator   He answers that people would see Moshe honoring himself and his family again and would complain that this was his own initiative. Therefore, to prevent this, he announced that G-d had instructed him to do so.

The *Sifsei Chachamim* (explaining *Rashi*) expounds further that although very soon the onlookers would understand that Moshe's instructions were directly from G-d, he did not want anyone to suspect him even for an instant. That is why he assembled everyone and told them these words before starting the process.

Q on the commentator   This *Rashi* with *Sifsei Chachamim* is puzzling. If Moshe was instructed straight from G-d to do something, why does he feel a need to explain himself? He knows he is doing the right thing with no ulterior motives. He is also an extremely busy man—teaching, adjudicating cases, and doing so much more. Why must he go out of his way to clarify himself to those who jump to conclusions and assume the worst?

New insight   We learn from this *Rashi* just how far our obligation extends to be transparent and clear up any possible suspicions that could potentially come up, even if they are unwarranted. Although Moshe was doing the right thing and knew it, and probably even felt deep down that he should not need to invest time or effort to defend himself, he knew the right thing to do was to go above and beyond in order to clear his name from any negative assumptions.

Lesson for life   This is an amazing concept that we often see in the Torah at both a communal and a personal level. At a communal level, the Jewish People are expected to do better and be a light onto the nations of the world. On a personal level, we are also held to a higher standard and must make every effort to show that we are above suspicion from anything that may appear to be improper, even if the observer is totally incorrect in his assumptions. May we merit to always make a *kiddush Hashem* (sanctification of G-d's name).

Rising to Our Potential

Dedication of this parashah is by the Zemmel Family

ויקרא ח:לו: וַיַּעַשׂ אַהֲרֹן וּבָנָיו אֵת כָּל הַדְּבָרִים אֲשֶׁר צִוָּה ה' בְּיַד
מֹשֶׁה:

גור אריה: להגיד שבחן. אלא שעשו זה בשמחה לקיים מה שאמר
להם משה כאילו שמעו מפי הגבורה. וזה יותר נכון, דזה שייך
כאן, כי דרך עולם—גדול שנצטווה מאחר, אינו עושה בשמחה
שהוא ישמע לאחר, אבל אהרן היה שמח כאילו בעצמו שמע.

P arashas Tzav says:

Aharon and his sons carried out all the matters that Hashem commanded through Moshe. (Vayikra 8:36)

Q on the verse Several commentators are bothered by why the Torah needs to mention this. Of course, Aharon and his sons did as they were told; they were spiritual giants and extremely righteous people.

A of the commentator The *Gur Aryeh* quotes the *Toras Kohanim*, which brings a novel approach. He comments that Aharon and his sons were being praised for not only doing as they were asked, but rather *how* they did those things. They did everything with *simchah* (joy)!

Q on the commentator

This *Gur Aryeh* is puzzling! Weren't Aharon and his sons constantly acting upon G-d's directions with great joy?

New insight

The *Gur Aryeh* is teaching that it is human nature that when someone receives instructions straight from the boss, he completes the task with more alacrity or joy. In this instance, Aharon could have asked, "Why didn't Hashem speak straight to me? *I'm* a prophet too!" He could have felt unmotivated (on some small level) to give it his all. Despite this, Aharon and his sons carried out the tasks they received "through Moshe" as if Hashem had spoken straight to them. And they did it with great joy, just as they would have done those tasks had Hashem commanded them directly to do them.

Lesson for life

Many times, we fall victim to our ego. "Why didn't he tell me that directly? Why did I have to get that information from an intermediary? Am I not important enough?" As a result, we do not do the great things of which we are capable. This could have happened to Aharon—one of the greatest people of all time. He was praised for negating his ego and doing the right thing. Let us each rise above pettiness and achieve greatness.

SHEMINI

Staying Laser-Focused

לעילוי נשמת צבי הירש בן אהרן יעקב, שרה פרידא בת משה
Dedicated by Rabbi and Mrs. Shmuel and Rikki Stein

ויקרא ט:ה: וַיִּקְחוּ אֵת אֲשֶׁר צִוָּה מֹשֶׁה אֶל פְּנֵי אֹהֶל מוֹעֵד וַיִּקְרְבוּ
כָּל הָעֵדָה וַיַּעַמְדוּ לִפְנֵי ה':

תרגום יונתן: וְאִזְדְּרִזוּן אַהֲרֹן וּבְנוֹי וְכָל בְּנֵי יִשְׂרָאֵל וּנְסִיבוּ יַת מַה
דְּפַקֵּיד מֹשֶׁה וְהַיְיתִיו לְקֳדָם מַשְׁכַּן זִמְנָא וּקְרִיבוּ כָּל כְּנִשְׁתָּא וְקָמוּן
בְּלֵב שְׁלִים קֳדָם ה'.

Parashas Shemini speaks about the Tabernacle and the offerings brought there.

They took what Moshe had commanded *to the front
of the Tent of Meeting; and the entire assembly approached and stood before Hashem. (Vayikra 9:5)*

The *Targum Yonasan* says that "**they took what Moshe had commanded**" is really highlighting and praising Aharon, his sons,
and the Jewish People for getting involved in the Tabernacle
"with alacrity and with a full heart."

Q on the
commentator This is a perplexing statement. Weren't they eager to participate in the building and offerings of the new Tabernacle, which would become the holiest place on earth? This is where G-d would perform daily miracles and where one would feel His presence and be able to draw closer to Him. Also, this temporary Temple in the desert would atone for them having worshipped the golden calf. Wouldn't they be motivated to jump into this project? So why the praise?

New
insight We learn from this *Targum Yonasan* an important life lesson. It is true that the people were excited to delve into this holy project for many reasons. We witnessed that motivation vividly when, as a result of their incredible enthusiasm to contribute so generously for "G-d's home on Earth," the fundraiser had to be stopped due to a surplus. Despite all this fervor, however, it is still extremely difficult to stay laser-focused on the goal at hand with zero distractions or ulterior motives. When we rise to the occasion and manage to accomplish such a thing, it is truly praiseworthy!

Lesson
for life Often, we become engrossed in projects that are truly commendable: helping someone in need, volunteering for a committee to run a dinner for the school or synagogue, or implementing a new idea that will help the community. We are passionate about the cause and want to make a difference. It is so important, however, not to divert any of that attention to honor, respect, or concerns for how we will be observed by others while doing such a great mitzvah. May we merit to utilize our time, effort, energies, and talents toward helping others wholeheartedly and selflessly!

Living Life Lessons

לעילוי נשמת יצחק בן יעקב, אליהו בן שמעון
Dedicated by Rabbi and Mrs. Shmuel and Rikki Stein

ויקרא י:ג: וַיֹּאמֶר מֹשֶׁה אֶל אַהֲרֹן הוּא אֲשֶׁר דִּבֶּר ה' לֵאמֹר בִּקְרֹבַי
אֶקָּדֵשׁ וְעַל פְּנֵי כָל הָעָם אֶכָּבֵד וַיִּדֹּם אַהֲרֹן:

דעת זקנים: בקרובי אקדש. על ידי מיתת קרובין הללו אתקדש
ואתגדל לעיני כל העם שישאו ק"ו בעצמם מאלו וישמרו עצמן
מלעשות כן וייראו ממני.

In *Parashas Shemini*, Nadav and Avihu, the sons of Aharon, brought a fire pan with incense before Hashem and died instantly. Some say they were punished for bringing an offering that was not warranted, and others say they entered the Holy of Holies when they were not supposed to.

> Moshe said to Aharon, "Of this did Hashem say, 'I will be sanctified through those who are nearest Me, thus I will be honored before the entire people.'" (Vayikra 10:3)

The *Daas Zekeinim* explains this verse to mean that Hashem was consoling Aharon. He was telling him that his sons did not die in vain. Rather, when people see that performing an unwarranted Temple service results in death, they will stop themselves from doing the same, however well-intentioned their motives may be.

The *Daas Zekeinim* is puzzling. Hashem warned the Jewish People more than once not to play with fire. There were many warnings not to ascend Mt. Sinai while G-d was giving the Ten Commandments. He also warned not to enter the Holy of Holies unless you are a High Priest and only on Yom Kippur. One of the jobs of the Levites was to guard the gates and warn people not to enter unless they were supposed to, lest they risk their lives. With all these warnings, do we really gain anything more by seeing two important Jewish rabbis killed?

We learn from this *Daas Zekeinim* that nothing is more powerful than seeing and experiencing a real-life example. *Rashi* brings a similar lesson regarding this incident in *Parashas Acharai Mos.* He says that if a sick person went to the doctor, and the doctor said, "Don't eat certain foods or sleep a certain way—because you might die," one might not take it so seriously. Yet, if the doctor says, "Don't eat certain foods or sleep a certain way—because you may die just like So-and-So died," one will take it much more seriously.

This lesson is powerful and real. Often, we may know a truism or an oft-repeated adage but fail to incorporate the lesson into our lives. The key is to learn a real-life example, allowing us to truly grow and avoid major pitfalls.

TAZRIA-METZORA

Hashem's Love for Us

*With great admiration and appreciation
to Rabbi Shimon Feder for your love and dedication
to teaching and guiding Jewish people and families.
Rabbi Noach and Chana Peled, North Miami Beach*

ויקרא יג:מז-מח: וְהַבֶּגֶד כִּי יִהְיֶה בוֹ נֶגַע צָרָעַת בְּבֶגֶד צֶמֶר אוֹ
בְּבֶגֶד פִּשְׁתִּים: אוֹ בִשְׁתִי אוֹ בְעֵרֶב לַפִּשְׁתִּים וְלַצֶּמֶר אוֹ בְעוֹר אוֹ
בְּכָל מְלֶאכֶת עוֹר:

רמב"ן: והבגד כי יהיה בו נגע צרעת ובתורת כהנים (מצורע פרשה
ה ג) דרשו עוד שאין הבית מטמא אלא לאחר כבוש וחלוק
ושיהא כל אחד ואחד מכיר ואת שלו והטעם כי אז נתישבה
דעתם עליהם לדעת את ה' ותשרה שכינתו בתוכם.

Parashas Tazria speaks about *tzaraas*, a terrible disease
caused by gossiping that used to afflict a person's body,
home, and clothing:

> *If there shall be a tzaraas affliction in a garment, in
> a woolen garment or a linen garment, or in the warp*

or the woof of the linen or the wool; or in leather or
in anything fashioned of leather…(Vayikra 13:47–48)

The commentator explains

The *Ramban* brings an interesting *Toras Kohanim*, which says that *tzaraas* only began once the conquest and division of land in Israel was complete and the feeling of G-d's presence among them was palpable. Before this took place (and nowadays), we are considered mentally "unsettled" and are not held to this higher standard. Therefore, G-d eradicated this illness.

Q on the commentator

This begs the question. If G-d deemed this spiritual disease as the appropriate consequence to the sin of gossip, why did he take it away just because we are "unsettled" today? Gossiping erodes relationships and can deeply hurt others. When *tzaraas* existed, G-d sent this illness as a clear and firm message for the sinner to stop, and he would be isolated from the rest of the camp for a "time-out" to reflect and repent.

New insight

This *Ramban* teaches us that G-d feels abundant compassion towards us and removed this punishment because even if we think we are fine today, our souls are not. In the past, G-d's presence was felt tangibly, and people recognized His hand in their lives, resulting in a certain serenity of the soul. Today, even if we are studying Torah, praying with fervor, and are blessed with success, deep down, our souls know something is missing. Without Mashiach and the Holy Temple, our souls feel unsettled.

G-d in His infinite *chessed* (kindness) negates this punishment for us, even when it should still be present.

Lesson for life

There are many examples in the Torah of G-d's love for us, such as how He counts the Jews in the beginning of the Book of Exodus right after He already counted us. The commentaries tell us that just as one counts and recounts his rare coin collection because it is beloved, so too, G-d is showing his love for us by counting and recounting us. It is so hard to go through life without a strong support system. Knowing that G-d created the world, loves us, and constantly looks for ways to do kindness with us—even when we do not notice—should uplift us in a major way.

This Too Shall Pass

In great love, honor, appreciation, and admiration
for our dear parents Rabbi Micha and Bracha Peled
and Dr. Eric and Bonni Lang.
Dedicated by Rabbi Noach and Chana Peled,
North Miami Beach

ויקרא טו:כה: וְאִשָּׁה כִּי יָזוּב זוֹב דָּמָהּ יָמִים רַבִּים בְּלֹא עֶת נִדָּתָהּ
אוֹ כִי תָזוּב עַל נִדָּתָהּ כָּל יְמֵי זוֹב טֻמְאָתָהּ כִּימֵי נִדָּתָהּ תִּהְיֶה
טְמֵאָה הִוא:

חזקוני: ימים רבים והלא אינן רק שלשה ימים אלא לפי שפורשת
מבעלה והם ימים של צער קורא אותם רבים.

Parashas Metzora tells us that if a woman has a *zava*-illness, she and her husband must separate for "**many days**."

Q on the verse The *Chizkuni* notes that the "**many days**" that the couple is required to separate for are only three days. Why then does the Torah call it "many days"?

A of the commentator   He answers that since the couple is going through a painful and challenging separation, albeit for only a short time, it feels like eternity.

Q on the commentator   This *Chizkuni* is difficult to comprehend. Why is the Torah emphasizing the waiting period? While we certainly understand the couple's angst, in reality it is only a few days.

New insight   We see from this *Chizkuni* a vital lesson. When one is going through difficulty, it truly feels like it will last forever, even if it is only temporary. The Torah recognizes this and is sensitive to these feelings.

Lesson for life   When going through a difficult time—whether it is sickness, loss of a loved one, or economic challenges—it feels like it will never end. The Torah is telling us that whenever we are going through difficult times, it will feel endless. But rest assured, one day it will end, and in hindsight, the challenge was just a short duration of time. Soon, we will be telling the next generation how we lived through this challenge and persevered. Like King Solomon wisely said, "This too shall pass."

ACHAREI-KEDOSHIM

Love over Hate

Dedicated by Rabbi and Mrs. Avraham Sussman
L'ilui nishmas their brother-in-law
Sholom Mordechai ben Tzvi, Reb Sholom Dreyfuss

ויקרא יט:יח: לֹא תִקֹּם וְלֹא תִטֹּר אֶת בְּנֵי עַמֶּךָ וְאָהַבְתָּ לְרֵעֲךָ
כָּמוֹךָ אֲנִי ה':

רש"י: לֹא תִקֹּם. אָמַר לוֹ הַשְׁאִילֵנִי מַגָּלְךָ, אָמַר לוֹ לָאו לְמָחָר
אָמַר לוֹ הַשְׁאִילֵנִי קַרְדֻּמְּךָ, אָמַר לוֹ אֵינִי מַשְׁאִילְךָ כְּדֶרֶךְ שֶׁלֹּא
הִשְׁאַלְתַּנִי, זוֹ הִיא נְקִימָה; וְאֵיזוֹ הִיא נְטִירָה? אָמַר לוֹ הַשְׁאִילֵנִי אֶת
קַרְדֻּמְּךָ, אָמַר לוֹ לָאו, לְמָחָר אָמַר לוֹ הַשְׁאִילֵנִי מַגָּלְךָ, אָמַר לוֹ הֵא
לָךְ, אֵינִי כְּמוֹתְךָ שֶׁלֹּא הִשְׁאַלְתַּנִי, זוֹ הִיא נְטִירָה, שֶׁנּוֹטֵר הָאֵיבָה
בְּלִבּוֹ, אַעַ"פִּי שֶׁאֵינוֹ נוֹקֵם. (ספרא; יומא כ"ג)

חזקוני: ואם תאמר מאי שנא שאין הקב"ה מזהיר בלאו על אותו
שלא רצה על לא דבר להשאיל לחבירו כליו ועל זה שיש לו
עליו טענה גדולה שלא רצה להשאילו תחלה הזהיר בלאו. וי"ל
שהראשון לא הניח להשאיל לו אלא מחמת צרות עין שהיה מגלו
חביב עליו ואין הקב"ה מכריחו להשאיל כליו שלא מרצונו אבל זה
שהיה משאיל לו לולי השנאה שהוא רוצה להנקם אם כן מחמת

129

שנאה הוא עושה כך לפיכך אמר הקב"ה תנצח האהבה שיש לך
עמו את השנאה שיש לך עמו ומתוך כך יבוא שלום בעולם.

Parashas *Kedoshim* says, "You shall not take revenge and not bear a grudge" (*Vayikra* 19:18).

Rashi says that if you ask to borrow a tool from a friend and he refuses, do not take revenge by refusing to lend to him when he is in need—and do not even bear a grudge by lending to him, albeit with resentment.

Q on the verse
Chizkuni asks, what about the first guy who would not lend anything to begin with?

A of the commentator
Answers the *Chizkuni*: Hashem does not fault the person who would not lend because he is always that way. But the second person *would have* lent out his things if he was not bearing "hatred towards him." Therefore, Hashem says, "Make victorious your love that you would have with him [over the hatred] and this will bring peace in the world."

Q on the commentator
This *Chizkuni* is troubling. At the present moment, the second individual, who was refused the tool he needed, has strong feelings of resentment against the one who did not lend him. How is it possible to overlook that?

New insight
The *Chizkuni* is teaching us that the Torah says you need to focus on the positive—in relationships, in friendships, in business, in everything. Every Jew is innately good, and we must remind ourselves of our power to tap into this powerful reservoir of love. We should not let frustrations with others from the past trump the way we react towards them in the future.

Lesson for life
This was an incredible attribute of the Novominsker Rebbe, who passed away recently. A major Jewish leader who got along with everyone, his boundless love for every Jew was immediately felt by all who encountered him. Today, let us rise above our frustrations with others, focus on love, and overpower any negative feelings we may be harboring. We should merit coming out of every situation stronger than ever with great relationships.

Knowing Is Half
the Battle

---

*Dedicated by Avraham Sussman in honor
of my longtime Chavrusa, Rabbi Shimon Feder*

ויקרא יט:לז: וּשְׁמַרְתֶּם אֶת כָּל חֻקֹּתַי וְאֶת כָּל מִשְׁפָּטַי וַעֲשִׂיתֶם
אֹתָם אֲנִי ה':

ספורנו: ושמרתם את כל חקותי ואת כל משפטי תעיינו בהם
ותכירו היותם הגונים ועשיתם אותם ובזה האופן תעשו אותם.

P arashas *Kedoshim* states: **"You shall observe all My
decrees and all My ordinances, and you shall perform
them**—I am Hashem" (*Vayikra* 19:37).

Q on the
verse *Sforno* is bothered by the Torah's redundancy in the verse. If
you are **"observing the decrees,"** isn't that the same thing as
"performing them"?

A of the
commentator He answers that this verse is a formula. **"You shall observe all
My decrees and all My ordinances"** teaches that if you delve
deeply into them and will recognize their value, then **"you will**

perform them," because you realize that they are good for you. If you do not appreciate the meaning, then you will not practice them.

This *Sforno* is difficult. We were given 613 commandments by the Master of the Universe and are obligated to do our utmost to fulfill them. Who cares if we do not value their importance?

We learn from this *Sforno* an amazing insight. Since we were given the understanding behind the mitzvos, there is more buy-in, and we appreciate them to a higher degree. Once we value them, we are ready to do them with more zeal. Even though we should be doing them regardless, human nature is to neglect directives when instructed without understanding why.

This holds true for everyone and everything in life. The *Sefer Hachinuch* wrote a comprehensive book for his children explaining the meaning and benefits of all the 613 mitzvos. One may ask, how did he interpret even those few mitzvos that we were not given the reasons for because G-d said they were beyond human comprehension? He explains that although we do not know the exact reasoning, we know some of the ways we benefit from these commandments, and knowing that is half the battle.

If we find ourselves lacking enthusiasm for performing some of the mitzvos, we should study the *Sefer Hachinuch* to help us get excited. If we have trouble encouraging our children, friends, or co-workers, we must recognize that if we will share how this project will benefit them and others, it will be the greatest motivator there is.

EMOR

Experiencing Judaism

Dedicated by David and Chaya Tova Hartman
in honor of Reuben Hartman. May he continue to be
a source of nachas to all who come in contact with him.

ויקרא כג:מא–מב: וְחַגֹּתֶם אֹתוֹ חַג לַה׳ שִׁבְעַת יָמִים בַּשָּׁנָה חֻקַּת
עוֹלָם לְדֹרֹתֵיכֶם בַּחֹדֶשׁ הַשְּׁבִיעִי תָּחֹגּוּ אֹתוֹ: בַּסֻּכֹּת תֵּשְׁבוּ שִׁבְעַת
יָמִים כָּל הָאֶזְרָח בְּיִשְׂרָאֵל יֵשְׁבוּ בַּסֻּכֹּת:

חזקוני: כל האזרח בישראל ישבו בסכת—חג זה נקבע בזמן
אסיפת גרן ויקב פן ירום לבבם על בתיהם שהם מלאים כל טוב
ויאמרו ידינו עשתה לנו את כל החיל הזה ומתוך שישבו בסוכה
יתנו שבח והודיה למי שנתן להם נחלה ובתים מלאים כל טוב.

Parashas *Emor* describes the curious commandment to
dwell in temporary booths during the holiday of Sukkos.

> *You shall dwell in booths for a seven-day period;* **every**
> **native in Israel shall dwell in booths.** *So that your*
> *generations will know that I caused the Children of*
> *Israel to dwell in booths when I took them from the*
> *land of Egypt...(Vayikra 23:41–42)*

133

Q on the verse — The *Chizkuni* wants to know why "**every native in Israel shall dwell in booths**"?

A of the commentator — He answers that we have a mitzvah to address our ego, which has been inflated by a successful harvest at this particular time of year. Therefore, G-d instructs us to humble ourselves by dwelling in booths (i.e., the sukkos) alone with Him under the stars.

Q on the commentator — The question on the *Chizkuni* is why the great scholar and leader Moshe could not have simply given the Jewish People a speech about it? He could have made a great cholent, served refreshments, and spoken during the harvest. If he felt that was too late and would not be as effective, he could have made a community-wide project for the month prior, giving out learning packets that discussed the evils of ego and over-inflated pride. Why the need to sit in the sukkah?

New insight — This amazing *Chizkuni* is teaching that although those ideas are beautiful and would be helpful on some level, they would not do the trick to counteract the arrogance that becomes embedded in us due to our success. Intellectually they may work, but emotionally they fall short. It is also not enough to only perform the mitzvos of shaking the Four Species and visiting G-d's presence at the Temple. We need the all-immersive experience of living in the sukkah and braving the elements, away from the comforts of home to truly connect to the meaning of this holiday.

Lesson for life — When we know something very well intellectually, we often feel that there is nothing needed to change or deepen our understanding. This could not be further from the truth. Just as we saw here, our religion is packed with rich experiences. Passover is another example. Why not just read a wonderful novel describing all that we went through and how grateful we are to be free? What's with all the symbolic food? The salt water reminds us of the tears they shed, while the bitter herbs how difficult their plight was. The real answer is, "**Knowing** is not believing, **experiencing** is."

The Power
of the Spoken Word

*Dedicated by David and Chaya Tova Hartman
in honor of Reuben Hartman. May he continue to be
a source of nachas to all who come in contact with him.*

ויקרא כד:יד: הוֹצֵא אֶת הַמְקַלֵּל אֶל מִחוּץ לַמַּחֲנֶה וְסָמְכוּ כָל הַשֹּׁמְעִים אֶת יְדֵיהֶם עַל רֹאשׁוֹ וְרָגְמוּ אֹתוֹ כָּל הָעֵדָה:

חזקוני: וסמכו מפני מה נתחייב זה סמיכה מכל חייבי מיתות לפי שבשעת גמר דין היו צריכים הדיינים לומר לעדים אמור בפירוש מה ששמעת והעדים אומרים בפירוש ברכת השם כמו ששמעו לכך היו סומכים את ידיהם עליו, כלומר העון הזה שאנו עושים לברך את השם יהא תלוי בצוארך שאתה גרמת לנו.

דעת זקנים: וסמכו כל השומעים. איתא בת״כ מה נשתנה מיתה זו שהיא בסמיכה אלא לפי שבשעת גמר דין צריכין העדים לומר בפי׳ כמו ששמעו מפי המברך לפיכך סומכין ידיהם עליו לומר העון הזה שאתה גורם לנו עליך יהיה.

135

Parashas *Emor* gives unusual instructions for those who heard someone curse G-d:

> Remove the blasphemer to the outside of the camp, and all those who heard **shall lean their hands upon his head**. *(Vayikra 24:14)*

Q on the verse   The *Chizkuni* and *Daas Zekeinim* ask: The Torah does not mandate us to lean our hands on any other sinner's head as judgment is meted out for any other transgression. Why is this case unique?

A of the commentator   They explain that the witnesses will be asked at the conclusion of the case to repeat the exact blasphemous words they had heard the offender previously utter. Placing their hands on the blasphemer's head seems to say, "The sin of this curse being uttered should not be attributed to us, rather it is upon him."

Q on the commentator   This explanation of theirs is difficult to understand. The witnesses are simply doing their civic duty. Why the need for theatrics (placing their hands on the sinner's head) as if to say, "He did this, not me?"

New insight   We learn an incredible insight from the *Chizkuni* and *Daas Zekeinim* that this action is more than just symbolism. Even repeating evil speech, when we are doing our duty to testify, has a negative spiritual impact on us, and we must do a prescribed action to counteract the effect this has on our soul.

Lesson for life   Speech has incredible spiritual power and can be harnessed for the good and the bad. We watch what we put into our mouth; we should watch what comes out of it.

Positive Influences

Dedicated by Moish and Doreen Mermelstein
L'ilui nishmas Chaim Aryeh ben Alexander

ויקרא כו:א: לֹא תַעֲשׂוּ לָכֶם אֱלִילִם וּפֶסֶל וּמַצֵּבָה לֹא תָקִימוּ לָכֶם וְאֶבֶן מַשְׂכִּית לֹא תִתְּנוּ בְּאַרְצְכֶם לְהִשְׁתַּחֲוֹת עָלֶיהָ כִּי אֲנִי ה' אֱלֹקֵיכֶם:

רש״י: לֹא תַעֲשׂוּ לָכֶם אֱלִילִים. כְּנֶגֶד זֶה הַנִּמְכָּר לְגוֹי, שֶׁלֹּא יֹאמַר הוֹאִיל וְרַבִּי מְגַלֶּה עֲרָיוֹת, אַף אֲנִי כְּמוֹתוֹ, הוֹאִיל וְרַבִּי עוֹבֵד עֲ״ז, אַף אֲנִי כְּמוֹתוֹ, הוֹאִיל וְרַבִּי מְחַלֵּל שַׁבָּת, אַף אֲנִי כְּמוֹתוֹ, לְכָךְ נֶאֶמְרוּ מִקְרָאוֹת הַלָּלוּ:

P arashas *Behar* discusses the grave sin of worshipping idols:

You shall not make idols for yourselves, and you shall not erect for yourselves a statue or a pillar, and in your Land you shall not emplace a flooring stone upon which to prostrate oneself—for I am Hashem, your G-d. (Vayikra 26:1)

Q on the
verse
Rashi is bothered by a question. We already know from the Ten Commandments and numerous places in the Torah that one must not worship idols. So why does the prohibition appear again here?

A of the
commentator
He answers that this verse is specifically addressing someone who sold himself into slavery under a non-Jewish master. Therefore, he may say to himself, "Since my master has illicit relationships, I will too. My master worships idols, I will as well. My master does not keep Shabbos, so will I break the Shabbos."

Q on the
commentator
This *Rashi* is difficult to digest. We are talking about a person who is a wholesome and seriously committed Jew, but who was down on his luck, so he made an arrangement with a non-Jew that included room, board, kosher food, and time off on Shabbos. How does witnessing his master doing these things influence him to do them as well?

New
insight
We learn from this *Rashi* the real power of foreign influences. If someone is keeping Shabbos, kashrus, attending Jewish schools, learning Torah, and doing all the mitzvos, yet witnesses others around him doing wrong, this environment can have a potent negative effect on him. Even though the non-Jewish master is not obligated to keep all the mitzvos, if a Jew witnesses his master doing these things, it can influence him to err in the worst sins possible.

Lesson
for life
The influences around us are stronger than we can imagine. We may try to convince ourselves that watching certain shows or spending time with the wrong people will not influence us poorly, but we are fooling ourselves. Everything has an impact on our psyche and can bring us down. Conversely, we learn from *Pirkei Avos* that even sitting and learning at the feet of the righteous can raise us to new heights. Let us always surround ourselves with positive people who will influence us to reach ever higher.

Knowing versus Feeling

Dedicated by Moish and Doreen Mermelstein
L'ilui nishmas Tzvi Elimelech ben Yisroel Yehuda

ויקרא כו:יג: אֲנִי ה׳ אֱלֹקֵיכֶם אֲשֶׁר הוֹצֵאתִי אֶתְכֶם מֵאֶרֶץ מִצְרַיִם
מִהְיֹת לָהֶם עֲבָדִים וָאֶשְׁבֹּר מֹטֹת עֻלְּכֶם וָאוֹלֵךְ אֶתְכֶם קוֹמְמִיּוּת:

רש״י: אני ה׳ אלקיכם. כְּדַאי אֲנִי שֶׁתַּאֲמִינוּ בִּי שֶׁאֲנִי יָכוֹל לַעֲשׂוֹת
כָּל אֵלֶה, שֶׁהֲרֵי הוֹצֵאתִי אֶתְכֶם מֵאֶרֶץ מִצְרַיִם וְעָשִׂיתִי לָכֶם נִסִּים
גְּדוֹלִים:

Parashas *Bechukosai* opens with all the blessings that come
to us if we follow in the ways of Hashem. The last verse
concludes: "**I am Hashem, your G-d, who took you out of the
land of Egypt from being slaves**…" (*Vayikra* 26:13).

Q on the verse *Rashi* is bothered by this. What is the purpose of reiterating the
well-known fact that Hashem took us out of Egypt?

A of the commentator *Rashi* answers that this verse emphasizes Hashem's complete
trustworthiness, as evidenced by the Exodus of Egypt and the
incredible open miracles He performed for us.

Q on the commentator   This *Rashi* is difficult to understand. What *new* piece of information did the verse impart? We already knew that Hashem took us out of Egypt! We are reminded of the Exodus at the Passover Seder, again within the *Shema*, and in our tefillin and mezuzah. We speak about these miracles and commemorate them often.

New insight   We learn from this *Rashi* that although it's evident that Hashem runs the world, sometimes we may *know* it, but don't *feel* it. Therefore, this simple reminder gives us strength and focus. (We find a similar lesson by Noach, who spent 120 years of his life building an ark yet still needed to be pushed on board by the waters of the flood.)

Lesson for life   Hashem loves us, provides for us, and is always with us. However, sometimes we lose sight of this fact when things are not going well. All we need is a gentle reminder: Hashem created the world, runs it, and sees the big picture. If He was able to change the world and economy during Egyptian times, He can certainly do it now.

Sefer Bamidbar

Dedicated by

Dr. William and Deborah Rand

in honor of our children

Dr. and Mrs. David and Rachel Rand

BAMIDBAR

All "Zoomed" Out?

Dedicated by Shani and Jordan Herman in memory
of Zalman Moshe ben Yosef Hacohein

במדבר א:יח: וְאֵת כָּל הָעֵדָה הִקְהִילוּ בְּאֶחָד לַחֹדֶשׁ הַשֵּׁנִי וַיִּתְיַלְדוּ
עַל מִשְׁפְּחֹתָם לְבֵית אֲבֹתָם בְּמִסְפַּר שֵׁמוֹת מִבֶּן עֶשְׂרִים שָׁנָה
וָמַעְלָה לְגֻלְגְּלֹתָם:

רמב"ן: ואת כל העדה הקהילו באחד לחדש השני יזכיר זריזות
משה רבינו במצות השם כי ביום הדבור לקח את הנשיאים והקהיל
כל העדה והתחיל לפקוד אותם אבל לא נשלם המנין ביום אחד
ולכך חזר ואמר (בפסוק יט) ויפקדם במדבר סיני להודיע שהיה
במקום ההוא המנין לא ביום ההוא.

In *Parashas Bamidbar*, Hashem commands Moshe to take a census in the desert shortly after leaving Egypt: "They gathered together the entire assembly on **the first of the second month**" (*Bamidbar* 1:18).

The *Ramban* is bothered by a question. Why does the Torah specify the date of this gathering?

143

A of the
commentator The *Ramban* answers that the Torah is noting Moshe's alacrity in performing the commandment of G-d. For on the very day of the Divine communication to Him, Moshe gathered the leaders and people and began to count.

Q on the
commentator This *Ramban* is troubling. Why is Moshe, a spiritual giant and legendary prophet, praised for doing as he was told without delay? What makes this special?

New
insight We learn from this *Ramban* that apparently, even Moshe, the ultimate *eved Hashem* (servant of G-d), could have easily rationalized or been lazy on some slight level. Between teaching Torah, consultations, and judgments, it was not so simple for him to drop everything and embark on a massive project. He pushed away that natural feeling of sluggishness and did not hesitate for a moment.

Lesson
for life Performing a mitzvah right away is not only praiseworthy, but we risk losing the golden opportunity altogether if it is pushed off. Sometimes, there is a natural tendency to become lethargic and tired. Seize opportunities for growth and introspection when they present themselves; you may walk away a completely different person. Let us use Moshe as a model to inspire us to have alacrity and accomplish remarkable things.

Numbers Matter!

Dedicated by Alon and Sarah Kamienny in honor of Rabbi Feder and all the JEC staff, past and present, for their efforts in bringing Torah to so many.

במדבר א:מה–מו: וַיִּהְיוּ כָּל פְּקוּדֵי בְנֵי יִשְׂרָאֵל לְבֵית אֲבֹתָם מִבֶּן עֶשְׂרִים שָׁנָה וָמַעְלָה כָּל יֹצֵא צָבָא בְּיִשְׂרָאֵל: וַיִּהְיוּ כָּל הַפְּקֻדִים שֵׁשׁ מֵאוֹת אֶלֶף וּשְׁלֹשֶׁת אֲלָפִים וַחֲמֵשׁ מֵאוֹת וַחֲמִשִּׁים:

רמב"ן: ויהיו כל פקודי בני ישראל לבית אבתם וגו' כל יצא צבא בישראל...ולא הבינותי טעם המצוה הזאת למה צוה בה הקב"ה כי היה צורך שיתיחסו לשבטיהם בעבור הדגלים אבל ידיעת המספר לא ידעתי למה צוה שידעו אותו אולי להודיעם חסדו עליהם כי בשבעים נפש ירדו אבותיהם מצרימה ועתה הם כחול הים.

I n *Parashas Bamidbar*, G-d commands Moshe to count each member of the Jewish nation.

> **These were the countings** of the Children of Israel, according to their fathers' households, from twenty years of age and up, everyone who goes out to the legion in

Israel. All their countings were six hundred and three
thousand, five hundred and fifty. (Bamidbar 1:45–46)

Q on the verse   *Ramban* poses a question. This mitzvah of counting six hundred thousand people must have been very taxing and time-consuming for Moshe and Aharon. What was the purpose of coming up with an exact number?

A of the commentator   He answers that it was necessary for the Jewish People to do this to help them fully appreciate the tremendous kindness of G-d. Just a few hundred years ago, as Yaakov and his family made their pilgrimage to Egypt, the Jewish People numbered only seventy people. Now, the men between twenty and sixty years of age alone numbered 603,550. We also know they used to give birth to sextuplets all the time! Hashem had created a huge nation out of just a few individuals. How grateful they were when they recognized G-d's kindness.

Q on the commentator   This *Ramban* sounds beautiful, but there is a basic question to ask. While it is true that it was a miraculous *chessed* of Hashem to watch our family expand greatly from seventy to 603,550, why is it necessary to know the exact number to appreciate this? Just the knowledge of this huge population growth should be sufficient to bring this point home!

New insight   We learn from this *Ramban* an important life lesson. Although we would sense the vast growth and feel grateful based on a solid estimate alone, it just would not be as effective as having the exact number. The real numbers give us concrete data to focus on and inspire us that much more.

Lesson for life   When my daughter was about to spend the holiday of Shavuos in Israel during her gap year of seminary, I reminisced about the incredible experience that I had had while spending time studying there:

Shavuos was the highlight of the year. After staying up the entire night studying Torah, we made our way to pray at the Western Wall, at the crack of dawn, along with thousands of Jews. As I walked with several friends, I turned around, seeing Jews making the same trek from every single direction for as far as the eye could see. It was truly an inspiring sight to behold!

As inspiring as it was, had someone given the exact statistics of how many were in attendance that day, it would have been even more impactful. Whenever a boss or co-worker nudges us for a number, we may find it annoying. They already have the big picture, why are they bothering me? The Torah tells us that besides the productivity angle, numbers really do make a difference.

NASO

The Source of All Blessings

Dedicated by Adam Fleischer in honor of the founders
of the East Boca Community and the Jewish Education
Center of South Florida. Thank you for sharing your
homes and your Torah with me.

במדבר ו:כד–כו: יְבָרֶכְךָ ה׳ וְיִשְׁמְרֶךָ: יָאֵר ה׳ פָּנָיו אֵלֶיךָ וִיחֻנֶּךָּ: יִשָּׂא
ה׳ פָּנָיו אֵלֶיךָ וְיָשֵׂם לְךָ שָׁלוֹם: וְשָׂמוּ אֶת שְׁמִי עַל בְּנֵי יִשְׂרָאֵל וַאֲנִי
אֲבָרֲכֵם:

חזקוני: ושמו את שמי הזכרת שמי בכל ברכה וברכה שיברכום
בשמי ולא בשמם היינו ואני אברכם לישראל שלא יהיו הכהנים
אומרים אנו נברך ישראל.

In *Parashas Naso*, Hashem tells Aharon that the Kohanim
will be a conduit to bless the Jewish People for all time by
administering the following blessings:

> *May Hashem bless you and safeguard you. May
> Hashem illuminate His countenance for you and be*

*gracious to you. May Hashem lift His countenance to you and establish peace for you. [The very next verse states:] Let them place **My name** upon the Children of Israel, and **I shall bless them**. (Bamidbar 6:24–27)*

Q on the verse This *Chizkuni* is bothered by the following: Why does the verse emphasize, "**My name**" and "**I shall bless them**"? We know that He is the source of all blessings and the Kohanim are only Hashem's messengers.

A of the commentator He answers that the Kohanim, who are entrusted with carrying out the important mission of blessing the people, may let it go to their heads that they are something special and that success is due to them. Therefore, Hashem reinforces the point: "It is really I Who blesses them."

Q on the commentator This *Chizkuni* is perplexing. Could it be that the Kohanim attributed the source of these blessings to themselves?

New insight We learn an incredible lesson from this *Chizkuni*. The Kohanim are immersed in a mitzvah as messengers of G-d, use language in each sentence that attributes these blessings to Him, and realize that physical and spiritual success comes from Him. Contrary to these three illustrations, they can still fall victim to their own ego.

Lesson for life As we look around at the crazy world today, let us not be deceived to think that we are ever in control of our livelihood, health, or safety. Rather, let us turn to the ultimate Source of blessing and ask Him to shower upon us all the blessings we need. Let us stay safe and healthy and work together to fight for a better future.

A Tinge of Jealousy

Dedicated by Adam and Tamar Fleischer in memory
of David Shakow, z"l who spread Torah learning
throughout his community and beyond

במדבר ז:יב: וַיְהִי הַמַּקְרִיב בַּיּוֹם הָרִאשׁוֹן אֶת קָרְבָּנוֹ נַחְשׁוֹן בֶּן
עַמִּינָדָב לְמַטֵּה יְהוּדָה:

רלב"ג: התועלת השמיני הוא במדות והוא להודיע שבדברים
אשר יהיה בהם כבוד למי שיהיה קודם אין ראוי לדקדק רק
בראשון שיהיה היותר נכבד אך אחריו לא נדקדק אלא לפי
מצבם ולזה התחיל נחשון בן עמינדב שהיה נשיא השבט היותר
נכבד להקריב קרבנו ואחריו נמשך העניין לפי המצב כדי שלא
תפול קנאה ביניהם בזה ולולי זה היה ראוי שיקריב נשיא שבט
ראובן אחר נשיא שבט יהודה כי ראובן היה הבכור והיה נופלת
קטטה ביניהם מי הוא היותר נכבד שבשבטים הם ואולם
כשנמשך העניין לפי מצבם סר המחלוקת והקנא' כי לא יתבאר
בזה שתהיה הקדימה מפני המעלה אבל מפני המצב.

Parashas Naso highlights the *nesi'im* (leaders) of each of the
twelve tribes by pointing out a special dedication offering
they each came up with independently of one another.

The one who brought his offering on the first day was
Nachshon, son of Amminadav, of the tribe of Yehudah.
(Bamidbar 7:12)

The commentator explains

The *Ralbag* tells us that Nachshon from the tribe of Yehudah was the most prominent, so he brought his offering first. After that, there was no rhyme or reason to the order; they all went according to how they encamped in the desert. The reasoning behind this "no order system" was because there would have been anger and jealousy among these leaders if the order were not totally random!

Q on the commentator

This *Ralbag* is hard to understand. The *nesi'im* were the most exalted Torah personalities of their time; they embodied wisdom and refined character traits. They were not looking for honor or respect. Furthermore, they were praised here for posterity because of their special offerings that they voluntarily dedicated to the Tabernacle. So, what was the concern here?

New insight

We learn from this *Ralbag* an unbelievable lesson. The Torah could have recorded the details of the offerings with the twelve leaders' names in just seven verses, thus giving them proper honor. Instead, the Torah mentioned each one separately, using seventy-two verses to give them incredible honor because they were truly deserving of it. Yet, despite all of this, had the leaders witnessed others going ahead of them in an order that was not by chance, these giants among men would have been upset and jealous of one another on some small level.

Lesson for life

Every day, we go to work or school and try to pretend that if others have been accorded admiration or honor while we have not, that it does not bother us at all. Just the opposite; we tell our friends that we are happy for them and their success. From this episode, we learn just how difficult it can be to eradicate these feelings. Let us realize this challenge and work on our *middos* and be truly happy for others.

BEHAALOSECHA

Equal Footing

---

*Dedicated by Dr. Sina and Mrs. Taly Menashehoff
in memory of Sina's father Dovid ben Avrohom*

במדבר י:ב: עֲשֵׂה לְךָ שְׁתֵּי חֲצוֹצְרֹת כֶּסֶף מִקְשָׁה תַּעֲשֶׂה אֹתָם וְהָיוּ
לְךָ לְמִקְרָא הָעֵדָה וּלְמַסַּע אֶת הַמַּחֲנוֹת:

רלב"ג: התועלת הה' הוא להודיע שראוי למנהיג העם והצבא
שתהיינה פעולותיו מסודרות באופן שלא תפול קטטה בין
המונהגים ממנו ולזה ראוי שיסדר עניין נסעם וחנותם ומי יסע
תחלה ומי יסע שני ומי יסע שלישי כי בזה מטוב הסדור וההרחקה
מהקטטה מה שלא יעלם.

Parashas *Behaalosecha* describes the system for alerting the entire Jewish nation when they would need to travel to the next stop in the desert during their forty years there. Hashem gave Moshe the following instructions:

> *Make for yourself two silver trumpets—make them hammered out, and they shall be yours for the summoning of the assembly and to cause the camps to journey. (Bamidbar 10:2)*

152

Q on the verse The *Ralbag* is bothered by a question. Why does the Torah detail how everyone was notified when it was time to pack up and move? What lesson do we learn from this?

A of the commentator *Ralbag* tells us that the Torah wanted this system to disseminate information to massive numbers of people simultaneously. Why? So that those who received the orders later were not jealous or angry that they were not notified earlier. Such is the responsibility of the leader to prevent any issues.

Q on the commentator The *Ralbag* is puzzling. Surely people understand that there is a hierarchy. Moshe set up such a tiered system for Torah teaching and judging cases. It was understood that Aharon and his sons were often privy to information first and that the leaders of the tribes and elders should learn of matters earlier. Even among those on a similar level, it is normal to assume that not everyone will always get the information at the same time. So why was it necessary to use this notification system? For the few people who would *kvetch* that they did not find out right away?

New insight We learn from this *Ralbag* a tremendous lesson. If we want to be great parents, teachers, or leaders, look for ways to provide everyone with information at the same exact time. Be creative in setting up systems so no one feels that someone got special attention, even if we think it is unnecessary or they are being overly sensitive. We must go out of our way and others will feel better about us, themselves, and the groups to which they belong.

Lesson for life Practically speaking, this can be difficult. We may be too busy and feel that people should just "grow up" and not let trivialities get to them. We may even be correct. Holding a leadership position, whether among family, friends, or on a project, brings with it tremendous responsibility. Let us step up to the challenge and reap the benefits that follow.

The Secret to Happiness

*Dedicated by Dr. Sina and Mrs. Taly Menashehoff
in memory of Taly's father Baruch ben Mordechai*

במדבר יא:א: וַיְהִי הָעָם כְּמִתְאֹנְנִים רַע בְּאָזְנֵי ה' וַיִּשְׁמַע ה' וַיִּחַר
אַפּוֹ וַתִּבְעַר בָּם אֵשׁ ה' וַתֹּאכַל בִּקְצֵה הַמַּחֲנֶה:

רבנו בחיי: ויהי העם כמתאוננים. מלשון (איכה ג':ל"ט) מה
יתאונן אדם חי, כי היו כואבים ומצטערים בהכנסם עתה במדבר,
והתאוננות זה היה רע באזני השם לפי שלא היו הולכים שמחים
אלא מוכרחים ודואגים. ואמר כמתאוננים בכ"ף הדמיון להורות
שהיו מגמגמין זה ולא היו מפרשין אותו מפני פחד משה כדי שלא
ישמע, ולכך אמר וישמע ה' כלומר ולא משה.

In *Parashas Behaalosecha*, Hashem punishes the Jewish People for their complaints in the desert:

> *The Jewish nation was **like complaining**; it was evil in the ears of Hashem. (Bamidbar 11:1)*

The Jews had been stationed at Mt. Sinai for a year and were told that they would have to start traveling around the desert. This stressed them out, and so they complained about their survival.

154

Rabbeinu Bachaya is bothered by the word *"k'misoninim,"* which translates literally to "**like complaining**." Did they complain or not?

He answers that the Jewish People did not complain directly to Moshe. Rather, they *kvetched* among themselves, as the verse says: "It was evil in the ears of Hashem." Rabbeinu Bachaya explains that even though the Jewish People did not launch an official grievance to Moshe, they were punished because they should have been *b'simchah* (overjoyed) with the miraculous bounty that Hashem was providing.

This explanation of Rabbeinu Bachaya is difficult to understand. Why did their behavior warrant punishment? They did not complain to Moshe like we find in many other places in the Torah. They were stressed and overwhelmed!

We learn from this Rabbeinu Bachaya an amazing life lesson. He explains that they were taken to task for their lack of gratitude. The miracles in the desert were extraordinary. The Well of Miriam quenched their thirst, and the manna provided food tasting like whatever they wanted delivered by "Hashem Prime." They had Clouds of Glory for temperature control and to clear the sands from venomous creatures, paving the roads and lighting the way. If they had only shifted their perspective, they would have been overwhelmed with gratitude.

We learn from here the powerful lesson that happiness is a conscious decision. There are countless miracles that surround us (perhaps less obvious than supernatural clouds and food) and acknowledging them is life-changing. By focusing on the good that surrounds us, we fill our hearts and minds with happiness, positivity, and fulfillment.

SHELACH

What Will
Your Legacy Be?

Dedicated by Sandy and Michael Lapkin
in memory of Anna and Sam Shapiro

במדבר יד:ב–ג: וַיִּלֹנוּ עַל מֹשֶׁה וְעַל אַהֲרֹן כֹּל בְּנֵי יִשְׂרָאֵל וַיֹּאמְרוּ
אֲלֵהֶם כָּל הָעֵדָה לוּ מַתְנוּ בְּאֶרֶץ מִצְרַיִם אוֹ בַּמִּדְבָּר הַזֶּה לוּ מָתְנוּ:
וְלָמָה ה׳ מֵבִיא אֹתָנוּ אֶל הָאָרֶץ הַזֹּאת לִנְפֹּל בַּחֶרֶב נָשֵׁינוּ וְטַפֵּנוּ
יִהְיוּ לָבַז הֲלוֹא טוֹב לָנוּ שׁוּב מִצְרָיְמָה:

חזקוני: הלוא טוב לנו שוב מצרימה כשהיינו במצרים אם מת אחד
ממנו היה מניח נכסיו לקרוביו או לשכניו אבל עכשיו הכל לבז.

I n *Parashas Shelach*, Hashem tells the Jewish People that He
will bring them to the land of Israel, a blessed homeland
flowing with milk and honey. But instead of joyfully accepting Hashem's gift, the people sent spies to check it out first.
Returning with a negative report, the spies persuaded the
Jewish People to be afraid and rebel against Hashem and Moshe.

156

[The nation cried out,] "If only we had died in the land of Egypt…Is it not better for us to return to Egypt?" (Bamidbar 14:2–3)

Q on the verse The *Chizkuni* is bothered by this. How could the Jewish People possibly long to return to the vile land where they were oppressed for generations?

A of the commentator He answers that if a Jew faced death in Egypt, his remaining possessions would be left with a relative or neighbor. But if the Jews entered Israel, they feared that they *all* would be wiped out completely with nothing left by which to be remembered.

Q on the commentator This *Chizkuni* is hard to understand. In Egypt, the Jews were slaves. What exactly did they own of true value? Probably not more than a pair of worn-out sandals!

New insight We learn that the fear of being completely forgotten is powerful. In Egypt, the Jews could at least leave a small item with someone, and they would be remembered by them. In their current scenario, they feared that they would be decimated by those living in Israel with no survivors. "Who will remember me? Who will care about those things that were important to me in my life?"

Lesson for life One of the most important things in one's life is his legacy. Deep down, everyone wants to impact the world and to be remembered by those around him. We have the power to make great things happen and make a lasting difference in this world. What will your legacy look like?

Facing Challenges

*Dedicated by Sandy and Michael Lapkin
in Memory of Estelle and Nat Lapkin*

במדבר יד:ט: אַךְ בַּה' אַל תִּמְרֹדוּ וְאַתֶּם אַל תִּירְאוּ אֶת עַם הָאָרֶץ
כִּי לַחְמֵנוּ הֵם סָר צִלָּם מֵעֲלֵיהֶם וַה' אִתָּנוּ אַל תִּירָאֻם:

רבנו בחיי: אַךְ בה' אַל תמרודו. למדך הכתוב שיראת העם הוא
מרד בהקב"ה.

In *Parashas Shelach*, the Jews approach the borders of the Land of Israel, which Hashem promised to be an amazing land flowing with milk and honey. The Jewish People are hesitant to proceed without sending spies to check it out, and Hashem agrees to their request. Upon their return, the vast majority of the spies speak ill about the Land and its inhabitants, instilling fear in the people by describing the giants living there. These spies persuade the people that they would never overtake their adversaries and would be signing their death warrants if they were to follow G-d's instructions to continue onward. However, the two spies who went against the others tried to encourage the nation to stay positive and to proceed onward to Israel.

The Jewish People, however, are told by one of the dissenting spies a different report:

> *"But do not rebel against Hashem! You should not fear the people of the Land...Their protection has departed from them; Hashem is with us. Do not fear them!" (Bamidbar 14:9)*

Q on the verse Rabbeinu Bachaya is bothered by a question. Why does it say, "**but do not rebel against Hashem**?" Did they take any action of rebellion? Did they pick up arms against Moshe or anyone else?

A of the commentator He answers that the verse is telling us "**do not rebel against Hashem**" by "**fearing the people of the Land.**" By the Jewish People harboring this fear, they were actually rebelling against Him.

Q on the commentator This Rabbeinu Bachaya seems harsh. If the Jewish People heard frightful horror stories and were afraid to confront giants, yet took no action against anyone, why were they faulted? How were their natural emotions considered a form of rebellion?

New insight We learn from this Rabbeinu Bachaya a new insight into our obligation as Jews. After Hashem had miraculously beaten the Egyptians with the ten plagues and then split the sea, and thereafter provided food and drink in the desert, just having this feeling of fear alone constituted a rebellion against G-d. Yes, the Jews heard a scary report, but by focusing on the knowledge of all that G-d had done for them, it was within their grasp to squelch that fear and proceed onward to Israel.

Lesson for life While we know intellectually that Hashem can do anything, it is extremely difficult to internalize this and put it into practice in our lives. Just as the Jews in the desert had an arsenal of faith that they could have tapped into, we too are given the tools to transcend each challenge in life and trust in G-d. If we focus in on all the times that Hashem has come through for us during difficulties, it can propel us to have faith in Him and not be fearful. This will give us peace of mind and tranquility to keep us going. Let us use this tool to strengthen ourselves in the face of life's challenges.

An Attitude of Gratitude

Dedicated by Karen Goliger in honor of her children
Alex, Myles, Max and Alexa

במדבר טז:טו: וַיִּחַר לְמֹשֶׁה מְאֹד וַיֹּאמֶר אֶל ה' אַל תֵּפֶן אֶל מִנְחָתָם לֹא חֲמוֹר אֶחָד מֵהֶם נָשָׂאתִי וְלֹא הֲרֵעֹתִי אֶת אַחַד מֵהֶם:

ספורנו: לא חמור אחד מהם נשאתי אפילו במה שיהנה הדיוט מחבירו לא נהניתי מהם שלא קבלתי מהם אפילו חמור בהשאלה ואם כן היתה שרדתי עליהם כולה לתועלתם ולתקן ענייניהם לא לתועלתי והנאתי כלל כמנהג כל משתרר ואינם מתרעמים על שרדתי אלא מצד מה שהם כפויי טובה.

In *Parashas Korach*, Korach, a well-respected figure in the community, led an uprising against his first cousins, Moshe and Aharon. He accuses them of a power grab, fueled by jealousy and resentment that Moshe appointed Aharon as the High Priest and his younger cousin, Elitzafon, as head of the Levites. Together with 250 firstborn men, Korach was able to start an uprising, as his congregation collectively felt that their positions to serve in the Tabernacle had been usurped, their honor unjustly stripped away from them, and what was rightfully theirs was given to the Levites.

> *This distressed Moshe greatly, and he said, "I have not taken even a single donkey of theirs, nor have I wronged even one of them." (Bamidbar 16:15)*

The commentator explains The *Sforno* expounds on Moshe's response, explaining that Moshe never even borrowed a donkey or used his position to benefit himself, even in an acceptable manner. "They only complained because they were *kafu'ei tovah* (deniers of the good) that was done for them."

Q on the commentator This is difficult to understand. What difference does gratitude make if this group felt deprived of honors which they deserved?

New insight We learn an amazing lesson from this *Sforno*. Had Korach and his entourage felt true gratitude towards Moshe, they never would have challenged him to begin with. They would have seen clearly that going up against Moshe was not the right move, ultimately saving their lives.

Lesson for life In life, it often feels like we are given the short end of the stick. Perhaps a coworker got that promotion that we felt we deserved, or a sibling was showered with praise when the credit should have gone to us. The Torah teaches us that the way to suppress these feelings is to tap into our feelings of *hakaras hatov* toward that person. Maybe that coworker went out of his way to guide you during your first week on the job, or perhaps that sibling is your best friend and has done things for you that no one else has done. When we recognize the debt of gratitude that we owe a person, such positive feelings can overcome any negative ones that stem from resentment.

Open Your Mind

*Dedicated by Karen Goliger in honor
of her bashert Michael Moed
and her mother Ann Cassouto, a true Aishet Chayil*

במדבר טז:ל–לג: וְאִם בְּרִיאָה יִבְרָא ה' וּפָצְתָה הָאֲדָמָה אֶת פִּיהָ
וּבָלְעָה אֹתָם וְאֶת כָּל אֲשֶׁר לָהֶם וְיָרְדוּ חַיִּים שְׁאֹלָה וִידַעְתֶּם כִּי
נִאֲצוּ הָאֲנָשִׁים הָאֵלֶּה אֶת ה': וַיְהִי כְּכַלֹּתוֹ לְדַבֵּר אֵת כָּל הַדְּבָרִים
הָאֵלֶּה וַתִּבָּקַע הָאֲדָמָה אֲשֶׁר תַּחְתֵּיהֶם: וַתִּפְתַּח הָאָרֶץ אֶת פִּיהָ
וַתִּבְלַע אֹתָם וְאֶת בָּתֵּיהֶם וְאֵת כָּל הָאָדָם אֲשֶׁר לְקֹרַח וְאֵת כָּל
הָרְכוּשׁ: וַיֵּרְדוּ הֵם וְכָל אֲשֶׁר לָהֶם חַיִּים שְׁאֹלָה וַתְּכַס עֲלֵיהֶם הָאָרֶץ
וַיֹּאבְדוּ מִתּוֹךְ הַקָּהָל:

רבנו בחיי: ותבקע האדמה אשר תחתיהם, ותפתח הארץ את
פיה ותבלע אותם. ותפתח הארץ את פיה, לבאר שהיה נס גדול
וענין כמוהו לא היה מעולם, שפתחה הארץ את פיה ובלעה אותם
ואח"כ נתכסה המקום, זהו שאמר ותכס עליהם הארץ, ואין זה
ענין טבעי, כי בבקיעת האדמה בקצת מדינות בנוהג שבעולם
אחר שהמקום ההוא מתבקע הוא נשאר פתוח, אבל בכאן אחר
הבקיעה הזכיר שפתחה הארץ את פיה ותבלע אותם וחזרה
לכסות עליהם, וזה היה נס גדול מן הנסים המפורסמים, ומפני
זה הזכיר הכתוב לשון בריאה, ואם בריאה יברא ה', שהוא לשון

163

המצא יש מאין, והענין המחודש הזה היה פלא עצום וחדוש גדול
כחדוש המצא יש מאין, עד כאן.

Parashas *Korach* talks about an uprising in the Jewish nation led by Korach. He was a wise leader with great oratory skills, who was also extremely wealthy. He utilized all these gifts to encourage many to join him, accusing Moshe of nepotism regarding some of the appointments that he had made.

Moshe warns Korach that if he continues in the path of *machlokes* (fighting), Hashem will bring a supernatural event to destroy him, his family, and all their worldly possessions.

> *"But if Hashem will create a **phenomenon**, and the ground will open its mouth and **swallow them** and all that is theirs, and they will descend alive to the pit—then you shall know that these men have provoked Hashem!"…They and all that was theirs descended alive to the pit; the earth **covered them over** and they were lost…(Bamidbar 16:30–33)*

Q on the verse

Rabbeinu Bachaya is bothered by a question. When Hashem comes to Moshe's aid here, why didn't he just bring several earthquakes for Korach and his clan to fall into? Why the need for a supernatural **"phenomenon"** that the world had never seen, leaving no trace of them and what had happened, as the ground **"swallowed them…and covered them over"** immediately after this event?

A of the commentator

He answers that had the people only witnessed these earthquakes, they would have rationalized that Korach was correct in his dispute against Moshe but was just unlucky to have been in the wrong place at the wrong time. Only when it was an unbelievable, never-before-seen event would the people be convinced of Korach's real guilt in his unwarranted accusations against Moshe.

Q on the
commentator

This Rabbeinu Bachaya is unbelievable. Despite all the miracles that Moshe had performed until now, coupled with what would have been a very precise warning of several earthquakes about to swallow Korach and his family simultaneously in twenty-five different places, this wouldn't have been enough to convince them?

New
insight

We learn from this Rabbeinu Bachaya an important lesson in human psychology. You can be experiencing the most miraculous things and yet be in denial of what is truly going on if it does not fall in line with your way of thinking. Therefore, G-d had to "trouble Himself" to do something so spectacular that the world had never seen in order to break through to them.

Lesson
for life

It is so difficult to change the patterns of thinking that are rooted in our culture, upbringing, political beliefs, and sphere of influence. Even when unusual things happen, they often fail to impact or change our way of thinking. Most people will share that during their lives they had something abnormal happen that shook them up and changed the course of their history. Let us learn to be open-minded to thinking differently by noticing when G-d sends a message our way.

CHUKAS-BALAK

Striking the
Proper Balance

Dedicated by Dr. and Mrs Dovid Goldschein
L'ilui nishmas Sara bas Harav Meshulam Feivish,
Harav Chaim Yoel ben Batsheva,
Freida bas Avrahom HaLevi

במדבר יט:כא: וְהָיְתָה לָהֶם לְחֻקַּת עוֹלָם וּמַזֵּה מֵי הַנִּדָּה יְכַבֵּס בְּגָדָיו וְהַנֹּגֵעַ בְּמֵי הַנִּדָּה יִטְמָא עַד הָעָרֶב:

חזקוני: והנגע במי הנדה יטמא תשובה למינים מה שפרה מטמאה כל העוסקים בה היינו טעמא לפי שהיא נעשית מחוץ למחנה ואם לא תטמא כל העוסקים בה חיישינן שמא יבואו בני אדם העושים עצמם פרושים ויקחו מעפרה ויזו על עצמם שלא לצורך ויאמרו רוצים אנו להיות טהורים ולכך צוה הכתוב שכל הטהורים הנוגעים בה יהיו טמאים.

Parashas *Chukas* starts out by talking about an unusual ritual. The red heifer is burned, and its ashes mixed with water are used to purify someone who had become impure.

166

At the same time that these ashes purify the impure person, they simultaneously—and contrary to logic—make the pure Kohen handling them impure!

> *This shall be for them an eternal decree. And the one who sprinkles the water of sprinkling shall immerse his clothing, and one who touches water of sprinkling shall be contaminated until the evening. (Bamidbar 19:21)*

The commentator explains The *Chizkuni* gives us the reasoning behind this. He says that if this process did not render the handlers of the ashes impure, then there would be *perushim* (holy people) who would want to use these ashes to purify themselves. Therefore, Hashem made a rule that anyone dealing with these ashes becomes impure.

Q on the commentator This sounds crazy. *Perushim* were special people who were steeped in spirituality and were genuine about keeping the Torah and mitzvos to the best of their abilities. So, if it was true that the ashes are pure and G-d made them impure to deter those from handling them when unnecessary, why not make a big announcement? Why not have Moshe give a class on all the details of purity, impurity, and the red heifer?

New insight The *Chizkuni* is sharing that apparently, this would not have been enough. G-d had to make the handler impure because there was no other plausible deterrent that would be effective at stopping such people. We know that many times, we should do more mitzvos and try to tap into more spirituality—yet we come up short. We see from here that one can be on the other end of the spectrum of holiness, sincerely driven to do the right thing, and yet, still go overboard. G-d did not change the rules for a few overzealous nuts; he changed them for good people who might otherwise get carried away. We must always work to strike a healthy balance.

Lesson for life This is applicable to everything in life. We must be balanced by focusing on our spiritual self while not neglecting the physical. During my gap year in Israel, my Rosh Yeshiva used to applaud those who exercised. He encouraged jumping rope, taking walks, and eating right. He lauded this as the Torah mandate of *"ve'chai bahem,"* i.e., "You should make sure to be living healthy by My commandments." Similarly, the *mussar* works speak about the importance of balance in every character trait. Usually, one should not be jealous or upset, but there is a time when it is proper. Study Torah and learn from the Divine book how to get the best out of life while striking the proper balance.

Productivity = Happiness

Dedicated by Dr. and Mrs Dovid Goldschein
L'ilui nishmas Sara bas Harav Meshulam Feivish,
Harav Chaim Yoel ben Batsheva,
Freida bas Avrahom HaLevi

במדבר כב:ו: וְעַתָּה לְכָה נָּא אָרָה לִּי אֶת הָעָם הַזֶּה כִּי עָצוּם הוּא מִמֶּנִּי אוּלַי אוּכַל נַכֶּה בּוֹ וַאֲגָרְשֶׁנּוּ מִן הָאָרֶץ כִּי יָדַעְתִּי אֵת אֲשֶׁר תְּבָרֵךְ מְבֹרָךְ וַאֲשֶׁר תָּאֹר יוּאָר:

ספורנו: אשר תברך מבורך הנה כחו לא היה לברך אבל היה לקלל בהזכיר עון או בכוון שעה כדברי רבותינו ז"ל ולכן לא שאל ממנו שיברכהו לנצח או שיוכל להתיצב מנגד אבל אמר ידעתי את אשר תברך מבורך לכבודו של בלעם להורות שלא חשב אותו למזיק בלבד

When Balak, the anti-Semitic king of Moav saw that the Jewish nation would ask to pass through his land on their way to Israel, he prepared for war. Knowing that Hashem would destroy anyone who sought to harm the Jewish People, he devised a two-pronged attack.

Balak implored Balaam, the powerful non-Jewish prophet, to try and weaken the Jewish nation, after which he would mobilize his army. Balaam's level of prophecy was on par with Moshe, and he knew the exact time of day that Hashem would allow curses to go through—even against His beloved nation.

Upon Balak hiring Balaam, the Torah states:

> *"Please come and curse this people for me, for it is too powerful for me; perhaps I will be able to strike it and drive it from the land. For I know that* **whomever you bless is blessed, and whomever you curse is accursed.***" (Bamidbar 22:6)*

Q on the verse
: The *Sforno* states that this verse is puzzling, because Balaam did not have the ability to bless, only to curse, and both Balak and Balaam knew this. If Balaam had the power to bless, Balak would have simply hired him to bless his army to become supersoldiers so that they could beat the Jewish People. Why, then, did Balak say, **"For I know whomever you bless is blessed,"** if it is not even true?

A of the commentator
: He answers that he said it "to give honor to Balaam, to show him that he didn't consider him as a *mazik* (destructive person) alone."

Q on the commentator
: This *Sforno* is hard to understand. It is nice of Balak to flatter Balaam with a false compliment, but they both knew the truth. So why did he say it if it was not true, and why did it help convince Balaam to take the position?

New insight
: The *Sforno* is teaching us that you can be wealthy, greatly respected, and on par with the greatest of prophets as Balaam was, but when the nature of your work is destructive and not productive, you will not be happy with yourself. Had Balak not falsely flattered Balaam for his ability to bless, he would not have been persuaded to take the job.

Lesson for life

A person has an innate need to live a productive life. Let us do some introspection as to what our G-d-given talents are. We have the tools to be productive and make an impact on the world around us. Through this, we will find true happiness.

PINCHAS

Who Is the Wise One?

Dedicated by Dovi Ettedgui in honor of his parents
Dr. and Mrs. Daniel and Rochelle Ettedgui

במדבר כז:ה: וַיַּקְרֵב מֹשֶׁה אֶת מִשְׁפָּטָן לִפְנֵי ה':

אבות דרבי נתן: ואינו בוש ללמד, זה משה שנאמר ויקרב משה
את משפטן לפני ה'. (שם כ"ז ה')

W hen Moshe was approached by the daughters of
Tzlafchad with a question regarding the laws of inher-
itance for the Land of Israel, he was unsure of the answer and
asked Hashem for help:

> "And Moshe brought their claim before Hashem."
> (Bamidbar 27:5)

Q on the verse
Avos D'Rabi Nosson is bothered by this. The Torah does not record every time Moshe asks Hashem a question, so why is this
specific episode highlighted?

A of the commentator
He answers that the verse is praising Moshe for not being afraid
to ask Hashem for help when he did not know the answer.

172

Q on the
commentator *Avos D'Rabi Nosson*'s commentary is puzzling. Why is Moshe praised for asking Hashem when he was unsure of the law? Isn't that what he was supposed to do?

New
insight

We learn from the *Avos D'Rabi Nosson* an amazing lesson—that even Moshe, the humblest of all men and the greatest prophet of all time, could have natural feelings of embarrassment on a slight level. It was commendable that he was able to push aside those feelings to clarify the Jewish law.

Lesson
for life

One of the most important ways to acquire wisdom is to not feel embarrassed to ask others for help. Sometimes, it may be difficult if you are supposed to know the answers. Other times, you may be older or more accomplished than someone in a particular field, and it is difficult to lower yourself and ask that person for help. The path to accomplishment and understanding is to never shy away from asking.

In *Pirkei Avos*, Ben Zoma says, "*Eizehu chacham ha'lomed mi'kol adam*—Who is the wise man? The one who learns from everyone" (*Avos* 4:1).

May we merit to learn from those around us, to never be embarrassed, and to grow as people.

Blinding Words

*Dedicated by Dovi Ettedgui in memory
of his dear grandfather Amram ben Shalom*

במדבר כז:ה: וַיַּקְרֵב מֹשֶׁה אֶת מִשְׁפָּטָן לִפְנֵי ה':

רבנו בחיי: ויקרב משה את משפטן לפני ה'. יש שפירשו כי כיון
שגלו בנות צלפחד בטענתן שלא היו אביהן מעדת שונאיו של
משה היה בזה קרוב הדעת למשה, ואלו היה דן את דינן היה
כאלו נוטל שחד דברים ועל כן חשך עצמו מן הדין ולא רצה
לדון אותן.

In *Parashas Pinchas*, the Torah speaks about the division
of Land that will take place when the Jewish People enter
Israel. The daughters of Tzlafchad approach Moshe and request
that the Land designated for their deceased father should go to
them because he had no sons to inherit him.

The Torah records that Moshe had to check in with G-d.

> *"Why should the name of our father be omitted from
> among his family because he had no son?" And **Moshe
> brought their claim before Hashem.** (Bamidbar 27:5)*

Q on the verse Rabbeinu Bachaya tries to figure out why "**Moshe brought their claim before Hashem.**"

A of the commentator His first approach is to say that Moshe wanted to recuse himself from answering them because the daughters mentioned that they were on his side regarding the dispute between him and Korach. He considered this a "bribe through words" with the potential to unduly influence him, and therefore, "Moshe brought their claim before Hashem" to avoid giving a biased ruling.

Q on the commentator This Rabbeinu Bachaya is puzzling. Moshe was of sterling character traits. He was the humblest man to walk the planet. Do we really think that he would let it go to his head that these women were on his side in the dispute, thereby impairing his ability to rule properly on the matter?

New insight We learn from this Rabbeinu Bachaya an amazing life lesson. Although it seems far-fetched that Moshe should be affected by this, he knew that these words could have impacted his judgment toward them, no matter how slightly, and that as a result, he needed to steer clear of deciding this case on his own.

Lesson for life Sometimes, we too are on the receiving end of flattery or approbations. They may not influence us on a conscious level, but without even knowing it, we may show favoritism towards that person in the future. Let us strive to steer clear of even a "bribe through words" and put honesty and integrity first in every given situation, just like Moshe.

Reaching New Heights

Dedicated by the Liberman family in memory
of Shifra Orlian a"h
Shifra Yehudis bas HaRav Nesanel Yosef tbldch"t

במדבר לא:ה-ו: וַיִּמָּסְרוּ מֵאַלְפֵי יִשְׂרָאֵל אֶלֶף לַמַּטֶּה שְׁנֵים עָשָׂר
אֶלֶף חֲלוּצֵי צָבָא: וַיִּשְׁלַח אֹתָם מֹשֶׁה אֶלֶף לַמַּטֶּה לַצָּבָא אֹתָם וְאֶת
פִּינְחָס בֶּן אֶלְעָזָר הַכֹּהֵן לַצָּבָא וּכְלֵי הַקֹּדֶשׁ וַחֲצֹצְרוֹת הַתְּרוּעָה בְּיָדוֹ:

דעת זקנים: וישלח אותם משה. הקב"ה אמר למשה נקום נקמת
אתה בעצמך והוא משלח אחרים אלא על ידי שנתגדל במדין
אמר אינו בדין שאבגוד בהם שהם עשו לי טובת הנאה כדאמרי
אינשי בירא דשתית מינה מיא לא תשדי ביה עפרא.

I n *Parashas Matos*, Hashem instructs Moshe to fight against
the Midianites, who harmed the Jewish nation in many ways.

*Moshe sent them—a thousand from each tribe, twelve
thousand armed for the legion: Pinchas lead them into
battle. (Bamidbar 31:5-6)*

Q on the verse The *Daas Zekeinim* and other commentators are bothered by a question: Why did Moshe send Pinchas to lead the men into battle if Hashem previously instructed *him* to gather the men to go to war?

A of the commentator The *Daas Zekeinim* answers that, "Moshe realized that it would be wrong to go into battle himself because he grew up in Midian and benefited from the nation. It would be traitorous to repay good with evil." As the saying goes, "The well that gave you to drink, don't throw dirt in it."

Q on the commentator This seems extreme considering the following circumstances:

- Nowhere does it say that the Midianites treated Moshe nicely during his sixty-year stay in Midian. Furthermore, the Midianites did not argue that the Jews should not attack them because Moshe had lived there once.
- The Midianites wanted to destroy Moshe's people and even caused a plague that wiped out twenty-four thousand Jews.
- Does it really make a difference if Moshe himself would go to battle? Wouldn't the resulting casualties be the same?

New insight We learn from this *Daas Zekeinim* a valuable lesson in gratitude, as demonstrated by Moshe. Although the Midianites deserved a reckoning, someone other than Moshe needed to be the one to carry it out. Living in their land for many years, Moshe had been the recipient of unintentional goodness. Therefore, he delegated the act of revenge for the sake of his own *middos* (personal growth). Such a nuanced level of sensitivity shows the extremely high level of character refinement toward which we should all be striving. (This lesson also appears during the ten plagues, when Moshe was instructed by God to delegate the striking of the Nile to Aharon as a sensitivity toward it, because the water had saved Moshe as a child.)

Lesson for life Although we are certainly not Moshe, we are to learn from him. It is important to not only exercise gratitude but to act upon it.

Ultimately, it is for our own benefit to recognize the good that others do, intentional or otherwise, because doing so will make us better spouses, better friends, and better human beings.

Getting Our Priorities Straight

*Dedicated by the Liberman family in memory
of Shifra Orlian a"h
Shifra Yehudis bas HaRav Nesanel Yosef tbldch"t*

במדבר לב:טז: וַיִּגְּשׁוּ אֵלָיו וַיֹּאמְרוּ גִּדְרֹת צֹאן נִבְנֶה לְמִקְנֵנוּ פֹּה
וְעָרִים לְטַפֵּנוּ:

במדבר לב:כד: בְּנוּ לָכֶם עָרִים לְטַפְּכֶם וּגְדֵרֹת לְצֹנַאֲכֶם וְהַיֹּצֵא
מִפִּיכֶם תַּעֲשׂוּ:

רש"י: נבנה למקננו פה. חָסִים הָיוּ עַל מָמוֹנָם יוֹתֵר מִבְּנֵיהֶם
וּבְנוֹתֵיהֶם, שֶׁהִקְדִּימוּ מִקְנֵיהֶם לְטַפָּם. אָמַר לָהֶם מֹשֶׁה "לֹא כֵן עֲשׂוּ
הָעִקָּר עִקָּר וְהַטָּפֵל טָפֵל, בְּנוּ לָכֶם תְּחִלָּה עָרִים לְטַפְּכֶם וְאַחַר כֵּן
גְּדֵרֹת לְצֹאנְכֶם". (תנחומא)

Parashas Matos speaks about the tribes of Reuven and Gad,
who had abundant livestock. They approach Moshe with
a request to remain on the other side of the Jordan River and
not participate in owning and settling in the Land of Israel.

When the tribes of Gad and Reuven were delineating the terms of the agreement, they stated:.

> They approached him and said, **"Pens for the flock shall we build here for our livestock, and cities for our small children."** (Bamidbar 32:16)

Just a few verses later, Moshe responds,

> **Build for yourselves cities for your small children and pens for your flock,** and what has come from your mouth you shall do. (Ibid. v. 24)

Q on the verse *Rashi* is bothered by a question. Why does Moshe switch the order of the **"pens for the flock"** and **"cities for the small children"**?

A of the commentator He answers that, by the fact that they mentioned pens for the flock first, Moshe perceived that they were more concerned about the welfare of their sheep than that of their children. Therefore, he reversed the order in his response in order to rebuke them, hoping to refocus their priorities as a result.

Q on the commentator This *Rashi* is hard to believe. How is it possible that they cared about their wealth more than their children? That sounds outlandish!

New insight We learn from this *Rashi* an astounding lesson. Indeed, such a thing is possible. They had been focused on their concern for their wealth and the welfare of their sheep while neglecting their beloved children. Moshe's response was teaching them that they lost sight of their priorities and needed to refocus.

Lesson for life If you were to stop someone on the street and ask him what is most important in life, of course the person would respond that his family comes first. We often witness people who love their family yet make their business the focal point of their lives to such a degree that they occasionally neglect those they hold dear. Let us never become distracted by our monetary pursuits and instead focus our attention on prioritizing spending time with those who are truly important to us!

Sefer Devarim

Constructive Criticism

Dedicated by Michael and Sylvia Kanoff and Family
(Miami Beach, FL)
in memory of Harry-Tzvi Kanoff (Yahrtzeit 15 Teves)

דברים א:א: אֵלֶּה הַדְּבָרִים אֲשֶׁר דִּבֶּר מֹשֶׁה אֶל כָּל יִשְׂרָאֵל בְּעֵבֶר
הַיַּרְדֵּן בַּמִּדְבָּר בָּעֲרָבָה מוֹל סוּף בֵּין פָּארָן וּבֵין תֹּפֶל וְלָבָן וַחֲצֵרֹת
וְדִי זָהָב:

רש"י: אֶל כל ישראל. אֵלּוּ הוֹכִיחַ מִקְצָתָן, הָיוּ אֵלּוּ שֶׁבַּשּׁוּק
אוֹמְרִים אַתֶּם הֱיִיתֶם שׁוֹמְעִים מִבֶּן עַמְרָם וְלֹא הֲשִׁיבוֹתֶם דָּבָר מִכָּךְ
וְכָךְ? אִלּוּ הָיִינוּ שָׁם הָיִינוּ מְשִׁיבִין אוֹתוֹ, לְכָךְ כִּנְּסָם כֻּלָּם וְאָמַר לָהֶם
הֲרֵי כֻּלְּכֶם כָּאן, כָּל מִי שֶׁיֵּשׁ לוֹ תְּשׁוּבָה יָשִׁיב. (ספרי)

Sefer Devarim opens with Moshe giving rebuke and then encouragement to the Jewish nation. He says that he is unable to cross the Jordan and enter the Land of Israel with them. He alludes to things they did wrong in the following places:

> These are the words that **Moshe spoke to all Israel**, on the other side of the Jordan, concerning the Wilderness, concerning the Aravah, opposite the Yam Suf, between

> *Paran and Tophel, and Lavan, and Chazeros, and Di-Zahav. (Devarim 1:1)*

Q on the verse

Rashi is bothered by a question. Why does it say "**Moshe spoke to all Israel**"? Did he really take upon himself the huge undertaking to assemble millions of people for this speech? And if so, why?

A of the commentator

He answers that Moshe understood that if he would have given this rebuke and not everyone was present, those who were not in attendance would say, "I can't believe you let Moshe talk to you like that! Had I been there, I would have responded to his reprimand." Therefore, he worked tirelessly to have **all of Israel** attend this assembly, and he indicated that if anyone had anything to retort, now was the time.

Q on the commentator

This *Rashi* is difficult to understand. It was common knowledge that over the last forty years in the desert, the Jewish nation had lost virtually all the people who were twenty years and up based on two major sins: the sin of the golden calf and the sin of the spies. Everyone had been directly affected by this, losing an older brother, parent, uncle, or other family member. What exactly could one who missed the program that day say?

New insight

We learn from this *Rashi* an important life lesson. While they knew intellectually there would have been nothing of significance to respond, they would nevertheless have had the feeling that they could have said something had they been there. This is because people have such a hard time hearing and accepting criticism—even when it is 100 percent true, and even from the greatest leader ever.

Lesson for life

We have a natural tendency to ignore rebuke or rationalize why we are correct. "They don't get it! If they understood the whole situation, they never would have said that to me!" When we ignore constructive criticism from others, we are putting aside an amazing tool that we can utilize in all pursuits in life. King Solomon said, "Like a ring of gold, a golden ornament, is a wise man's reproof in a receptive ear." Let us always be open to hearing how we can correct and better ourselves.

Why Me?

Dedicated by Michael and Sylvia Kanoff and Family
(Miami Beach, FL)
in memory of Harry-Tzvi Kanoff (Yahrtzeit 15 Teves)

דברים א:ג: וַיְהִי בְּאַרְבָּעִים שָׁנָה בְּעַשְׁתֵּי עָשָׂר חֹדֶשׁ בְּאֶחָד לַחֹדֶשׁ דִּבֶּר מֹשֶׁה אֶל בְּנֵי יִשְׂרָאֵל כְּכֹל אֲשֶׁר צִוָּה ה' אֹתוֹ אֲלֵהֶם:

רש"י: ויהי בארבעים שנה בעשתי עשר חדש באחד לחדש. מְלַמֵּד שֶׁלֹּא הוֹכִיחָן אֶלָּא סָמוּךְ לַמִּיתָה; מִמִּי לָמַד? מִיַּעֲקֹב, שֶׁלֹּא הוֹכִיחַ אֶת בָּנָיו אֶלָּא סָמוּךְ לַמִּיתָה, אָמַר, רְאוּבֵן בְּנִי אֲנִי אוֹמֵר לְךָ מִפְּנֵי מָה לֹא הוֹכַחְתִּיךָ כָּל הַשָּׁנִים הַלָּלוּ, כְּדֵי שֶׁלֹּא תַנִּיחֵנִי וְתֵלֵךְ וְתִדְבַּק בְּעֵשָׂו אָחִי.

מהרי"ק: פירוש רש"י שיעקב אמר לראובן בני אומר לך מפני מה כו. תימה מנא ליה לרשי שאמר יעקב כוליה האי? ואומר מהריק דמדקאמר ליה יעקב לראובן שהפסיד בכורתו על שסרח לקלקל יצועו בודאי היה ירא שמא ידבק בעשו שגם הוא היה מערער על הבכורה שהפסיד.

Devarim deals with Moshe's parting words to the Jewish People shortly before his death: "It was toward the end

185

of the fortieth year when Moshe spoke to the Children of Israel"
(*Devarim* 1:3), giving them final rebuke and instruction.

The commentator explains *Rashi* explains that Moshe waited decades to rebuke them before
he died so that they would accept the rebuke wholeheartedly.
He learned this lesson from our forefather Yaakov, who admonished his eldest son Reuven this way. Had Yaakov done it earlier,
Reuven may have left home and joined his evil uncle, Esav.

The *Maharik* (1420–80) further expounds upon *Rashi*, stating
that Yaakov told his son he lost his firstborn status. He feared
Reuven would be embittered and seek solidarity with his uncle,
who also held a grudge for losing his firstborn status. The patriarch Yaakov deeply understood human nature, and he knew this
outcome was a real possibility.

Q on the commentator These commentaries are puzzling. Other than two transgressions, Reuven was righteous. The Talmud tells us that Esav
committed heinous sins, including rape and murder (*Bava
Basra*). So why on earth would Reuven join *him*, one of the evilest men of the generation?

New insight *Rashi* shows us an important lesson in human psychology.
Everyone, including the most virtuous individual, has a powerful, innate desire to be understood—and may even go to the
extreme to find someone who identifies with him. This desire
runs so deep that even Reuven—one of the twelve tribes—could
have justified joining his evil uncle to fulfill this emotional need.

Lesson for life This has great relevance today. Many times, we go through
a difficult challenge, asking ourselves, "Why me?" We all face
struggles of different kinds, and overcoming them equips
us with the tools to help others cope with similar situations.
Having been in their shoes, we can understand those people in
a way that no one else can. When we empathize and let them
know that we "get them," we provide them with the necessary
strength and inspiration to pull through. Let us turn challenges,
difficulties, and hardships into tools for helping others.

VA'ESCHANAN

Hidden Agendas

*Dedicated by David and Chaya Tova Hartman
in honor of Sonny Hartman. May he continue to be
a source of nachas to all who come in contact with him.*

דברים ד:כב: כִּי אָנֹכִי מֵת בָּאָרֶץ הַזֹּאת אֵינֶנִּי עֹבֵר אֶת הַיַּרְדֵּן
וְאַתֶּם עֹבְרִים וִירִשְׁתֶּם אֶת הָאָרֶץ הַטּוֹבָה הַזֹּאת:

חזקוני: איננו עבר את הירדן ויש לכם להתבונן כי לא לצרכי אני
אומר לכם לשמור את המצות.

I n *Parashas Va'eschanan*, Moshe prepares the Jewish People
for his departure from them with some final directives and
instructions.

> *"For I will die in this land; I am not crossing the
> Jordan—but you are crossing and you shall possess
> this good land." (Devarim 4:22)*

Chizkuni is bothered by a question. Why is the verse stressing,
"I am not crossing the Jordan?" We already know that Moshe
will not continue with the Jewish People into the Land of Israel.

187

A of the commentator

He answers that Moshe was really telling them to deeply contemplate the following fact: "I, Moshe, never told you to keep the mitzvos for my sake. It is only for your benefit. Therefore, continue to keep them once I am gone."

Q on the commentator

This *Chizkuni* is hard to understand. We know that G-d gave the Jewish nation the mitzvos for their benefit, and it had nothing to do with Moshe. They had previously proclaimed, "*naaseh v'nishma*," accepting the Torah wholeheartedly because they understood its value. So how could they possibly think that it was for Moshe's benefit?

New insight

We learn from the *Chizkuni* a most valuable insight into human nature. The people knew intellectually that the mitzvos were beneficial for them and for their relationship with G-d. They also understood that the commandments helped them stay rooted in morality, ethics, and growth. Despite all this, on some level, they pushed back. This is because it is human nature to dislike being forced into doing things, even when we know deep down that it is good for us. This is especially true if there may be an agenda of the one encouraging such things. And that is why Moshe had to tell them, "The mitzvos are good for you always, even when I will no longer be here or pushing you."

Lesson for life

Our campus rabbi, who has inspired so many, told me the following: He often meets up with students who would like a relationship with G-d and the Torah. Some have been inspired to start learning and connecting, while others are simply curious if there is more depth to Judaism than what they experienced in Hebrew School. Every so often, a student will come to him and say, "I know Torah and Judaism is good for me in so many ways, but I ran away from my last mentor. This was because I sensed he had an agenda. When I come to study Torah with you, I know that you only want what is best for me. That is why I continue coming!" Let us always make sure to help people and inspire them for their sake alone, conveying Moshe's message.

The True Reality

*Dedicated by David and Chaya Tova Hartman
in honor of Sonny Hartman. May he continue to be
a source of nachas to all who come in contact with him.*

דברים ד:כה–כו: כִּי תוֹלִיד בָּנִים וּבְנֵי בָנִים וְנוֹשַׁנְתֶּם בָּאָרֶץ
וְהִשְׁחַתֶּם וַעֲשִׂיתֶם פֶּסֶל תְּמוּנַת כֹּל וַעֲשִׂיתֶם הָרַע בְּעֵינֵי ה' אֱלֹהֶיךָ
לְהַכְעִיסוֹ: הַעִידֹתִי בָכֶם הַיּוֹם אֶת הַשָּׁמַיִם וְאֶת הָאָרֶץ כִּי אָבֹד
תֹּאבֵדוּן מַהֵר מֵעַל הָאָרֶץ אֲשֶׁר אַתֶּם עֹבְרִים אֶת הַיַּרְדֵּן שָׁמָּה
לְרִשְׁתָּהּ לֹא תַאֲרִיכֻן יָמִים עָלֶיהָ כִּי הִשָּׁמֵד תִּשָּׁמֵדוּן:

דעת זקנים: כי תוליד. כלו' שתאמרו כבר נתישבנו בארץ ולא
ירבה עוד כעס והשחתה הנני מעיד עליכם דברים שהם קיימים
לעולם דהיינו שמים וארץ כי אבוד תאבדון ולא יועיל לכם מה
שנתישבתם בה.

חזקוני: ונושנתם בארץ ותהיו נואשים ותאמרו כבר נתישבנו בה
ולא נפסידנה עוד.

In *Parashas Va'eschanan*, Moshe warns the Jewish People:

*"When you will have children and grandchildren and
will have been long **settled in** the land, you may become*

> *corrupt and make idols which will anger Hashem.*
> *I appoint heaven and earth on this day to bear witness*
> *against you and you will be kicked out of My land..."*
> *(Devarim 4:25–26)*

The commentator explains

The Torah is telling us that future generations may begin to succumb to the temptation of idol worship. The *Daas Zekeinim* and *Chizkuni* explain that had Moshe not given this intense warning, the people would not have believed that the Holy Land would spit them out because they had "**settled in**" the land for a long period of time.

Q on the commentator

This is puzzling. If they believe that Hashem will punish them and kick them out of the land if they worship idols, what difference should it make that they have "settled in"? Would a landlord ever tell a tenant who is about to be evicted, "Never mind, I see that you've settled in for several years and have a lot of stuff, so I won't bother evicting you even though you've violated our lease agreement."

New insight

The *Daas Zekeinim* and *Chizkuni* are teaching us that even if you believe in Hashem and His consequences, you will have a hard time believing the situation can change based on the reality that you are used to. "I live in the land. I send my kids to this school. I go to work. I have my group of friends. These things aren't going to change!"

Lesson for life

If someone had ever predicted several months ago that the world would be turned upside-down, people would be afraid to go to the store, synagogues would shut their doors, and the economy would be in shambles, we would have called them crazy! No matter how comfortable we have become in our current situation, the status quo can turn around in an instant.

The only thing we can be completely certain of is Hashem's total control over our *reality*. Let us work on doing more mitzvos, prayer, and Torah learning, and may they be a merit for Hashem to give us a reality of health, prosperity, and friendship. Let us enjoy a world where we can always travel to see friends and relatives, one where we can recharge and reconnect with Him at the Western Wall and never again take these things for granted.

EIKEV

Providing for Our Needs

*Dedicated by Andrea and David Dolny in memory
of Andrea's father Tzvi Hershel Hillel ben Avraham, z"l
כ"ג אב צבי הרשל הלל בן אברהם ז"ל on his 50th Yahrzeit*

דברים ח:ג: וַיְעַנְּךָ וַיַּרְעִבֶךָ וַיַּאֲכִלְךָ אֶת הַמָּן אֲשֶׁר לֹא יָדַעְתָּ וְלֹא
יָדְעוּן אֲבֹתֶיךָ לְמַעַן הוֹדִעֲךָ כִּי לֹא עַל הַלֶּחֶם לְבַדּוֹ יִחְיֶה הָאָדָם כִּי
עַל כָּל מוֹצָא פִי ה' יִחְיֶה הָאָדָם:

חזקוני: וירעיבך שלא נתן לך מן אלא דבר יום ביומו וזהו וירעבך
שאינו דומה מי שיש לו פת בסלו למי שאין לו פת בסלו.

חזקוני: ה' אלקיך מיסרך שלא הושיט לך מזון לכמה ימים בפעם
אחת פן תמרוד בו אלא מזון לפרנסת היום כדי שיהו עיניך תמיד
תלויות בו.

After forty years spent wandering the desert, Moshe
recounts to the Jewish People: "Hashem let you **hunger**
and then He fed you the manna…" (*Devarim* 8:3)

Q on the verse

The *Chizkuni* is bothered by a question. Why does the verse say
that Hashem let them "**hunger**" if He provided sufficient manna
to eat every day?

192

A of the
commentator

He answers that although the manna arrived daily and completely satiated their hunger, they were left with nothing extra
to store at home. This was the hunger that the Torah was referring to. Why did Hashem operate with this system of hunger?
He did not want us to be too comfortable, for if we had "bread in
the basket", we wouldn't have full faith in Him and we may even
rebel against Him (*Chizkuni*, v. 5).

Q on the
commentator

This *Chizkuni* is difficult to understand. He is saying that had
Hashem sent us manna from heaven every Sunday morning for
the entire week, we would feel comfortable that there's food in
the pantry and, on some level, lose our impetus to pray as hard
to Him for sustenance. Not only would we drop in our level of
faith and connection to Him, but we may have even become
rebellious. Really?

New
insight

We learn from this *Chizkuni* an unbelievable lesson for life. With
all the open miracles the Jewish People experienced daily in the
desert for forty years, they still needed to exercise their mus-
cles of faith and reliance on Hashem daily. Although the Well
of Miriam gave water for three million people, temperature-
control clouds illuminated and cleared the path for travel, and
the manna tasted like whatever food you liked best, if you have
money in the bank or food in the fridge, you don't turn to
Hashem the same way. If today was a rough day and I did not
pray so well, I may say, "Don't worry G-d, I don't need your help
today, I have leftovers from yesterday."

Lesson
for life

We learn from the lesson of the manna that no matter how
little we may have or how uncertain the markets are, Hashem
will always be there for us. We just need to recognize that He is
providing all our needs daily. He yearns for us to connect with
Him—whether by way of formal prayers or by just speaking to
Him using our own words. Ultimately, He will provide for all
our needs.

True Value

Dedicated by Andrea and David Dolny in memory
of Andrea's father Tzvi Hershel Hillel ben Avraham, z"l
כ״ג אב *on his 50th Yahrzeit* צבי הרשל הלל בן אברהם ז״ל

דברים יא:יד: וְנָתַתִּי מְטַר אַרְצְכֶם בְּעִתּוֹ יוֹרֶה וּמַלְקוֹשׁ וְאָסַפְתָּ דְגָנֶךָ וְתִירשְׁךָ וְיִצְהָרֶךָ:

ברכות לה ע״ב: תָּנוּ רַבָּנַן: ״וְאָסַפְתָּ דְגָנֶךָ״ מַה תַּלְמוּד לוֹמַר?—לְפִי שֶׁנֶּאֱמַר: ״לֹא יָמוּשׁ סֵפֶר הַתּוֹרָה הַזֶּה מִפִּיךָ״—יָכוֹל דְּבָרִים כִּכְתָבָן, תַּלְמוּד לוֹמַר: ״וְאָסַפְתָּ דְגָנֶךָ״—הַנְהֵג בָּהֶן מִנְהַג דֶּרֶךְ אֶרֶץ, דִּבְרֵי רַבִּי יִשְׁמָעֵאל. רַבִּי שִׁמְעוֹן בֶּן יוֹחַאי אוֹמֵר: אֶפְשָׁר אָדָם חוֹרֵשׁ בִּשְׁעַת חֲרִישָׁה, וְזוֹרֵעַ בִּשְׁעַת זְרִיעָה, וְקוֹצֵר בִּשְׁעַת קְצִירָה, וְדָשׁ בִּשְׁעַת דִּישָׁה, וְזוֹרֶה בִּשְׁעַת הָרוּחַ, תּוֹרָה מַה תְּהֵא עָלֶיהָ? אֶלָּא בִּזְמַן שֶׁיִּשְׂרָאֵל עוֹשִׂין רְצוֹנוֹ שֶׁל מָקוֹם—מְלַאכְתָּן נַעֲשֵׂית עַל יְדֵי אֲחֵרִים, שֶׁנֶּאֱמַר: ״וְעָמְדוּ זָרִים וְרָעוּ צֹאנְכֶם וְגוֹ׳״, וּבִזְמַן שֶׁאֵין יִשְׂרָאֵל עוֹשִׂין רְצוֹנוֹ שֶׁל מָקוֹם—מְלַאכְתָּן נַעֲשֵׂית עַל יְדֵי עַצְמָן, שֶׁנֶּאֱמַר: ״וְאָסַפְתָּ דְגָנֶךָ״.

מהרש״א: שנאמר ואספת דגנך וגו׳. יש לעיין בזה דהיאך מתוקם האי קרא ואספת דגנך וגו׳ באין עושין רצונו של מקום הא מפורש ביה והיה אם שמוע וגו׳ לאהבה את ה׳ וגו׳ ועלה קאי ונתתי מטר

194

וגו' ואספת דגנך וגו' והיפך באין עושין רצונו של מקום השמרו
לכם פן וגו' ולא יהיה מטר וגו' וי"ל בזה כדברי התוספות דודאי
איירי קרא בעושין רצונו של מקום. אבל אין עושין רצונו כ"כ
דאינן צדיקים גמורים דאע"ג דכתיב ביה והיה אם שמוע וגו'
לאהבה וגו' מכל מקום מדכתיב בהך פרשה בכל לבבכם ובכל
נפשכם ולא כתיב נמי ובכל מאדכם כדכתיב בפרשת שמע ובכל
מאדך משמע ליה דאיירי הכא באינן צדיקים גמורים דהיינו
שאינם צדיקים במאד כדאמרינן דיש לך אדם שחביב לו ממונו
יותר מגופו.

P *arashas Eikev* brings the second paragraph of the *Shema*, which describes the reward of those who listen to G-d.

Then I shall provide rain for your land in its proper time, the early and the late rains, that you may **gather in your grain**, *your wine, and your oil. (Devarim 11:14)*

The Talmud tells of a dispute regarding one's obligation to work. Rabbi Yishmael said that although one may have thought to spend all day in spiritual pursuits, "**gather in your grain**" teaches that a person must go to work. Rabbi Shimon Bar Yochai said one should spend all day in spiritual pursuits, and "gather in your grain" refers to one who has failed to reach this high level of faith. Therefore, a person such as this, who has failed to reach this level, must exert much effort by working (*Berachos* 35b).

Q on the verse
The *Maharsha* asks how can Rabbi Shimon Bar Yochai say this verse implies something negative when the Torah was listing all the blessings for one who keeps the commandments?

A of the commentator
He answers that even Rabbi Shimon Bar Yochai would agree that this verse is mainly positive, but it is referring to a righteous individual who has not yet reached the pinnacle of his faith in Hashem. He infers this from the contrast between the first and second paragraphs of the *Shema*. The first paragraph states, "You shall love Hashem with all your **heart,** with all your **soul,**

and with all your **resources**." The second states, "with all your **heart** and with all your **soul**." What happened to **resources**? From here, the *Maharsha* concludes that these were righteous people who were willing to give their lives for G-d, yet on some level, loved their resources even more than their lives and were not willing to sacrifice those.

This *Maharsha* is hard to believe. How is it possible for a person to be so dedicated while loving G-d, willing to sacrifice his heart and soul, yet unwilling to forgo his resources?

We learn from this *Maharsha* an unbelievable lesson. One can be so dedicated that he is even willing to give up his life, yet when challenged with surrendering his money, he just cannot bring himself to do it.

If we were to ask anyone what he values more, his money or his life, he would immediately and unequivocally answer: life is more important. And yet, despite this sentiment, we can still relate to the story of the man who received a dire prognosis from his doctor and was told that if he did not cut back on his hours at the office that he would end up with a heart attack. Nevertheless, the man was back to his old habits in no time, eventually winding up in the hospital. Let us value what has true worth over what has secondary value, and let us live a life of happiness and fulfillment.

RE'EH

Building Boundaries

Dedicated in loving memory of Nathan, Lillian,
and Marc Sabshon

דברים יב:יג: הִשָּׁמֶר לְךָ פֶּן תַּעֲלֶה עֹלֹתֶיךָ בְּכָל מָקוֹם אֲשֶׁר תִּרְאֶה:

חזקוני: השמר לך פן תעלה וגו׳ מה שהחמיר הכתוב כל כך
לאסור הבמות משנבנה בית עולמים היינו שעל ידי הבמות גרמו
להם לישראל שנמנעו לעלות לרגל ומזבחים ומקטרים בבמות,
ומשהתחילו לזבוח ולקטר בבמות עוד הוסיפו למעול מעל לזבוח
ולקטר לעגלים שבבית אל ושבדן.

Parashas Re'eh discusses the Jewish law that once the
Temple was built, one was no longer permitted to bring
an offering on a private altar.

*Beware of yourself lest you bring up your elevation-
offerings **in any place that you see**. (Devarim 12:13)*

Q on the
verse

The *Chizkuni* wants to know the reasoning behind this prohibition. Doesn't it sound like a wonderful idea to bring an offering
wherever we find ourselves, not just at the Temple?

197

A of the commentator The *Chizkuni* gives two answers. The first is that practically speaking, if everyone could bring his offering in his backyard or a public park, he would no longer come to visit in the Temple during the holidays because it would be more convenient to stay at home. Second, once he starts bringing offerings outside the Temple, he will continue by bringing offerings to idols.

Q on the commentator This *Chizkuni* is difficult to comprehend. His first answer makes a lot of sense. It is akin to opening in-home prayer groups all over, preventing the need for people to attend synagogues. However, the second answer is very strange. You have someone expending time, effort, energy, and money trying to do a beautiful mitzvah. Why are we concerned that he will switch his modus operandi and start doing one of the cardinal Jewish sins?

New insight We learn from this *Chizkuni* a shocking truth about human nature. Even if one goes through the motions with the intention of doing a big mitzvah, but can now easily utilize the same materials and similar actions to do a sin, he may take this opportunity to try it. His curiosity—coupled with the desire to worship idols—may put him over the edge. This is true even when committing one of the most heinous sins in the Torah. That is why the Torah makes a *geder* (an extra boundary) that we should not make or use an altar outside the Temple.

Lesson for life Although the desire for worshipping idols has mainly disappeared and we have no proclivities toward such worship, there are still many things in life that beg for our attention and to which we may easily fall prey to. For this very reason, the Torah sometimes has an extra layer of prohibition to protect us. Along the same lines, the Torah may have permitted a certain action around which the rabbis later enacted a prohibition, ensuring an extra measure of help for us for all time. One such example of this was the prohibition of not eating milk and chicken together. This was set up to prevent us from ever coming to eat milk and meat together, which can be quite similar in appearance. Let us look toward the Book of the Torah, which teaches us how to get the best out of life and which can train us not only to protect ourselves, but to grow as well.

Love Will Change
Our World

*Dedicated in loving memory of Nathan, Lillian,
and Marc Sabshon*

דברים יד:א: בָּנִים אַתֶּם לַה׳ אֱלֹקֵיכֶם לֹא תִתְגֹּדְדוּ וְלֹא תָשִׂימוּ
קָרְחָה בֵּין עֵינֵיכֶם לָמֵת:

דעת זקנים: בנים אתם לה׳ אלהיכם. ולכן אם מת אביכם הבשר
ודם לא תתגודדו שהרי אינכם יתומים בכך כי יש לכם אב
שהוא חי וקיים יתברך וית׳ שמו אבל העכו״ם כשמת אביו יש
לו להתגודד שאין לו עוד אב כי אם עצו ואבנו שאין בם מועיל
כדכתיב אומרים לעץ אבי אתה ולאבן את ילדתנו:

Parashas Re'eh tells us:

You are children to Hashem, your G-d—**you shall
not cut yourselves** and you shall not make a bald spot
between your eyes for a dead person. (Devarim 14:1)

Q on the verse Many commentators are bothered by a question. What is the correlation between **"You are the children to Hashem"** and **"you shall not cut yourselves"**?

A of the commentator The *Daas Zekeinim* explains that we are commanded to abstain from cutting ourselves when grieving a lost parent or relative, which was once a common display of mourning, because we are Hashem's children. Although it is heartbreaking to lose a family member, and we may feel depressed and alone in the world, we must know that we are not orphaned completely, so our grieving should be reduced accordingly. Our loving Father in Heaven still loves us and watches out for us.

Q on the commentator This *Daas Zekeinim* is hard to relate to. Perhaps the loftiest rabbis of the generation can feel this way, but can the average Jew? How can we feel the love of Hashem to the same degree as a flesh-and-blood parent? Our parents woke up in the middle of the night to comfort us, they fed us, bathed us, supported us emotionally, physically, and financially. Can we really feel that an intangible G-d supports and loves us the same way?

New insight We see from this *Daas Zekeinim* that even though Hashem is not a physical being asking us how our day went, it is possible to feel His loving presence and appreciate all that He does for us every day. In fact, this is a commandment incumbent upon every Jew. Each of us can tap into Hashem's love and internalize the reality that He is here for us at every moment like a father who checks on his children.

Lesson for life The Torah says that one should never torment a widow or an orphan because Hashem will hear their cries and step in "as a husband or father would" to punish those who harassed his children.

We must know and recognize that Hashem is always watching out for our best interests and cares for us more than we can ever imagine. All we must do is open our hearts and minds to connect with Him. If we think about this daily, it will change our world.

SHOFTIM

Too Blessed
to Be Stressed

Dedicated by Leene and Bob Chavez
to our children Andrew, Ken, Howard, Jenna,
and to their spouses and children

דברים כ:ה: וְדִבְּרוּ הַשֹּׁטְרִים אֶל הָעָם לֵאמֹר מִי הָאִישׁ אֲשֶׁר בָּנָה
בַיִת חָדָשׁ וְלֹא חֲנָכוֹ יֵלֵךְ וְיָשֹׁב לְבֵיתוֹ פֶּן יָמוּת בַּמִּלְחָמָה וְאִישׁ
אַחֵר יַחְנְכֶנּוּ:

רש״י: וְאִישׁ אַחֵר יחנכנו. וְדָבָר שֶׁל עָגְמַת נֶפֶשׁ הוּא זֶה.

שפתי חכמים: ודבר של עגמת נפש הוא זה. דאל״כ מאי נפקא
מיניה אם יחנכנו הוא או אחר.

In *Parashas Shoftim*, we learn of an unusual exemption from
serving in the Jewish army:

> *Who is the man who has built a new house and has not*
> *inaugurated it? Let him go and return to his house, lest*
> *he die in the war **and another man will inaugurate it.***
> *(Devarim 20:5)*

202

Rashi is bothered by a question. Why is this man bothered that **"another man will inaugurate it?"** Shouldn't he be more concerned that he may die?

Rashi, as expounded by *Sifsei Chachamim*, explains that this draftee worries that he will never be able to live in his new property and that someone else will inhabit it if he dies in battle. His fear renders him unable to focus properly on the war, and as a consequence, he is exempt from the draft.

This *Rashi* begs the question: How could a person be more preoccupied with someone enjoying his brand-new home than the fear of losing his life and never seeing friends or family again? He risks never again witnessing a beautiful sunrise, interacting with loved ones, or making a difference in the world. Aren't these things more important?

We learn from this *Rashi* an incredible insight into human nature. Although logically one should be more stressed about losing his life in battle, thoughts of jealousy can dominate his conscience. The thought that someone else will live on to enjoy *his* property, dine at *his* table, and sleep in *his* bed can totally consume a person. His jealousy causes him to be distracted, which exempts him from duty. Jealousy is so powerful that a person can be concerned about what will be with his possessions even after his death.

It is important to focus on the true priorities in our lives. Life is a gift, and we are here on earth for an exalted purpose. Avoiding being jealous of others is the key to true happiness and getting the most out of life. As Ben Zoma says in *Pirkei Avos*, "Who is rich? He who rejoices in his lot."

Powerful Influences

Dedicated by Leene and Bob Chavez
to our children Andrew, Ken, Howard, Jenna,
and to their spouses and children

דברים כ:יח: לְמַעַן אֲשֶׁר לֹא יְלַמְּדוּ אֶתְכֶם לַעֲשׂוֹת כְּכֹל תּוֹעֲבֹתָם
אֲשֶׁר עָשׂוּ לֵאלֹהֵיהֶם וַחֲטָאתֶם לַה' אֱלֹקֵיכֶם:

רמב"ן: וטעם אשר לא ילמדו אתכם לעשות ככל תועבתם אשר
עשו לאלהיהם וכאן הוסיף לבאר שלא תחיה כל נשמה כי אפילו
היחיד הנשאר ביניכם לעבוד לך יזכיר לך עבודתם לאלהיהם
ואולי תתפתה אתה לעשות כן לשם הנכבד ותחטא לפניו יתברך.

In *Parashas Shoftim*, the Torah speaks about removing the evil influences of the other nations while the Jews are settling into the Promised Land of Israel.

> So that they will not teach you to act according to all their abominations that they performed for their gods, so that you will sin to Hashem, your G-d. (Devarim 20:18)

Q on the verse The *Ramban* here references the previous verse, which tells us to remove or destroy every single one of these people and wants to know why it is necessary to go to such an extreme. Can one individual really influence us?

A of the commentator He answers that it was imperative to remove all bad influencers around us per G-d's instruction because they could sway a person to worship idols and perform other abominations.

Q on the commentator This *Ramban* sounds like an exaggeration. Let us assume the Jewish People settle into a city with their synagogues, Jewish schools, and kosher eateries. They are connected spiritually and physically to G-d and a robust and growing Jewish community. Do you really think that if one idolatrous guy is still around, he can negatively impact people in any real way?

New insight We learn from this *Ramban* just how powerful and impactful those around us can be. We can start out doing all the right things for the right reasons, yet having a non-Jewish neighbor steeped in idolatry can influence us negatively. A single person—even one with whom we are not close and even one whom we do not admire in the slightest or hold in any kind of esteem—any person can profoundly impact our actions. Therefore, the Torah warns us that we must be proactive to get rid of him.

Lesson for life In life, we are constantly exposed to a variety of people who can shape who we are. Whether it be friends, family, co-workers, or the person we see occasionally, everyone has the potential to bring us down or lift us up. Let us surround ourselves with great role models and always act in a manner that positively impacts those around us.

KI SEITZEI

Culture of Kindness

*Dedicated by Judy and Michael Kaiser in loving memory
of Moshe Chuna Kaiser of blessed memory*

דברים כג:ד–ה: לֹא יָבֹא עַמּוֹנִי וּמוֹאָבִי בִּקְהַל ה' גַּם דּוֹר עֲשִׂירִי
לֹא יָבֹא לָהֶם בִּקְהַל ה' עַד עוֹלָם: עַל דְּבַר אֲשֶׁר לֹא קִדְּמוּ אֶתְכֶם
בַּלֶּחֶם וּבַמַּיִם בַּדֶּרֶךְ בְּצֵאתְכֶם מִמִּצְרָיִם וַאֲשֶׁר שָׂכַר עָלֶיךָ אֶת
בִּלְעָם בֶּן בְּעוֹר מִפְּתוֹר אֲרַם נַהֲרַיִם לְקַלְלֶךָ:

רש"י: עַל דבר. עַל הָעֵצָה שֶׁיָּעֲצוּ אֶתְכֶם לְהַחֲטִיאֲכֶם.

שפתי חכמים: על העצה כו'. דאל"כ ל"ל דבר, הל"ל אשר לא
קדמו וגו'. אלא ה"ק קרא על הדיבור כלומר על העצה אשר לא
קדמו וגו', כלומר ובשביל דבר זה נמי. ור"ל דאשה, כמו ואשר.

P arashas *Ki Seitzei* explains why the men of the Amonite
and Moabite nations are prohibited from marrying
a Jewish woman:

> *An Amonite or Moabite shall not enter the congrega-
> tion of Hashem...to eternity. Because of the fact they
> did not greet you with bread and water on the road*

206

when you were leaving Egypt, and because they hired
Balaam, son of Beor, to curse you. (Devarim 23:4–5)

The commentator explains According to *Rashi* (as expounded by *Sifsei Chachamim*), there are three reasons these nations are banned from **ever** marrying in:

1. They listened to the advice of Balaam to get the Jewish People involved in illicit relationships, ultimately causing a plague that claimed twenty-four thousand lives.
2. They did not display the proper etiquette of offering food and water to the Jews as they passed through their land.
3. They hired Balaam to curse the nation as an attempt to destroy them.

Q on the commentator This *Rashi* is puzzling. The first and third reasons given to exclude an Amonite or Moabite appear to be justified. They attempted and later succeeded in wiping out many of our people both spiritually and physically. The middle reason, however, seems illogical. The nations showed poor etiquette and lacked appropriate *chessed* (kindness) by withholding food and drink. But why does this exclude them from ever marrying a Jewish woman?

New insight We learn from this *Rashi* that lacking basic *chessed* is no small matter! Amazingly, it is on par with the other two wicked crimes committed by the Amonite and Moabite people. If a person is unaccustomed to kindness and his base nature is selfish, he lacks a core element of the Jewish soul. Because of this, he will not be able to marry into the Jewish nation—ever. As the Talmud in *Yevamos* (78b) says: All of Avraham's descendants will inherently possess three qualities: modesty, compassion, and **kindness.**

Lesson for life To be a Jew is to tap into this inner wellspring of *chessed*. Recently, Jews worldwide raised two million dollars in five days for a baby in Florida who needed one of the world's most expensive drugs. In Jewish communities, you can visit a free-loan fund called a *gemach* (an acronym for *gemilus chassadim,* "acts of kindness") for almost anything—clothing, medical supplies, books, and equipment, to name a few. When there is a birth, death, or trauma, families arrange to cook meals and offer support of every kind. Hatzalah has thousands of Jewish volunteer emergency medics worldwide. Kindness is within the very spiritual DNA of the Jewish People and the essence of the Torah itself.

Let us practice tapping into our hallmark trait of *chessed* in any way that we can, finding ways to provide for what others are lacking—be it a kind word, something to eat, something to wear, a job, or even a marriage partner.

Feeling for Others

*Dedicated by Judy and Michael Kaiser in loving memory
of Moshe Chuna Kaiser of blessed memory*

דברים כד:יח: וְזָכַרְתָּ כִּי עֶבֶד הָיִיתָ בְּמִצְרַיִם וַיִּפְדְּךָ ה' אֱלֹקֶיךָ מִשָּׁם
עַל כֵּן אָנֹכִי מְצַוְּךָ לַעֲשׂוֹת אֶת הַדָּבָר הַזֶּה:

חזקוני: וזכרת כי עבד היית כשתזכור בעצמך שהיית עבד כבר
וצריך לאחרים תרחם על גר יתום ואלמנה ולא תטה משפט.

T he Torah tells us how careful a judge must be not to per-
vert the judgment of a convert, an orphan, or a widow.

> *You shall remember that you were a slave in Egypt,
> and Hashem, your G-d, redeemed you from there;
> therefore, I command you to do this thing. (Devarim
> 24:18)*

Q on the
verse

Chizkuni is bothered by a question. How do the words, "**you
shall remember that you were a slave in Egypt**" explain why
one should be careful with the judgment of the downtrodden?

A of the commentator He answers that when one remembers that we were once slaves, downtrodden and needy, we will have compassion for the convert, widow, and orphan. Only then will we give them an unaltered and true judgment.

Q on the commentator This *Chizkuni* is puzzling. Everyone understands that if a person can identify with someone personally, he will go the extra mile and have more patience, working even harder to do the right thing. It has been thousands of years since we were slaves, so how is it possible for us to feel like we were in that situation when we really don't remember what it was like? Passover is about feeling that experience, but it is very difficult to do! Shouldn't we just be commanded to have extra compassion for the convert, widow, and orphan because it is the right thing to do?

New insight We learn from this *Chizkuni* an important lesson in life. Although we must make every effort to judge the convert, widow, and orphan fairly, trying to do the right thing for them is not enough. We must put ourselves in that person's shoes, feeling his suffering and the fact that he is all alone in the world. Only then can we help the downtrodden to the utmost degree. And this is done by using our memory and imagination of what happened to us so many years before.

Lesson for life It is very difficult to use imagery and imagination to feel for others, yet we know that if we can tap into this, we can have more empathy for people. This will bring our relationships to new depths and allow us to help others at the high level they deserve. We can feel their pain and suffering, and join with them in their sorrow. The great Rabbi Aryeh Levine once accompanied his wife to the doctor. When the doctor asked, "What seems to be the problem?" The rabbi answered, "Doctor, our foot hurts us." Let us use this tool to strengthen our relationships with others.

KI SAVO

Appreciating
Our Treasure

*Dedicated by Floris and Murray Leipzig in memory
of their parents Bill and Ellen Gordon Leipzig
and Herbert and Clara Unger Schoenfeld*

דברים כו:כו: אָרוּר אֲשֶׁר לֹא יָקִים אֶת דִּבְרֵי הַתּוֹרָה הַזֹּאת לַעֲשׂוֹת אוֹתָם וְאָמַר כָּל הָעָם אָמֵן:

רמב"ן: אשר לא יקים את דברי התורה הזאת ולי נראה על החזן שאינו מקים ספר תורה על הצבור להראות פני כתיבתו לכל כמו שמפורש במסכת סופרים (יד יד) שמגביהין אותו ומראה פני כתיבתו לעם העומדים לימינו ולשמאלו ומחזירו לפניו ולאחריו שמצוה לכל אנשים והנשים לראות הכתוב ולכרוע ולומר וזאת התורה אשר שם משה וגו' (לעיל ד מד) וכן נהגין.

In *Parashas Ki Savo*, we deal with certain sins that get a curse in addition to the regular punishment:

*Accursed is the one who will not **uphold the words of this Torah** to perform them. (Devarim 27:26)*

211

Q on the verse Many commentators are intrigued by this. It cannot mean that a person is cursed for not upholding any of the Torah laws, as the Torah only mentions a select few deserving of a curse. What then, is the meaning behind this verse?

A of the commentator *Ramban* answers: "Cursed is the leader who didn't **uphold the Torah** to show the letters properly. As the halachah tells us that one who lifts the Torah must also open the scroll and move to the right and to the left to allow all to see it and recite 'V'zos HaTorah'…"

Q on the commentator This *Ramban* is hard to relate to. The Torah lists idolatry, immorality, and harassing a blind person as terrible sins incurring curses. Why does one who improperly performs the *hagbah* (lifting of the Torah) become cursed? How does failing to showcase the letters of the Torah fall into the same category of major crimes?

New insight We learn a vital lesson from this *Ramban*. While it is certainly true that this action is not on par with the others, it is in the category of something very wrong. Tractate *Sofrim* goes into extensive detail about the laws of honoring the Torah. If we do not **uphold the Torah** and honor it properly, and instead diminish its honor to all those viewing it, we are committing a major offense and not a minor one.

Lesson for life The Torah was given exactly 3,334 years ago. It is not only the instruction manual for how to get the best out of life but it is what connects us to the Creator of the universe. It has many levels of understanding. Like an onion, Torah can be peeled back to reveal layer after layer of depth. Someone can learn a page of Talmud in his youth, again in his adolescence, and again when he is much older, constantly discovering new ideas hidden beneath the surface. To delve into its study is the biggest mitzvah.

G-d's Torah is the treasure of the Jewish People. Let us cherish it and show our deepest respect for this gift by honoring it, living by it, and studying it.

Overriding Fear

דברים כח:ס: וְהֵשִׁיב בְּךָ אֵת כָּל מַדְוֵה מִצְרַיִם אֲשֶׁר יָגֹרְתָּ מִפְּנֵיהֶם
וְדָבְקוּ בָּךְ:

רש"י: אשר יגרת מפניהם. מִפְּנֵי הַמַּכּוֹת. כְּשֶׁהָיוּ יִשְׂרָאֵל רוֹאִין
מַכּוֹת מְשֻׁנּוֹת הַבָּאוֹת עַל מִצְרַיִם, הָיוּ יְרֵאִים מֵהֶם שֶׁלֹּא יָבֹאוּ גַם
עֲלֵיהֶם.

Parashas *Ki Savo* enumerates the reward that will come to
the Jewish People if we perform G-d's mitzvos and, conversely, the punishments if we do not.

> *He will bring back upon you all the sufferings of Egypt,*
> **of which you were terrified**...(Devarim 28:60)

Rashi is bothered by a question. What does the phrase "**of
which you were terrified**" mean in the past tense? Shouldn't it

say "of which the Egyptians were terrified" or "that you will be terrified" in the future?

A of the commentator
He answers that the verse is teaching that the Jewish People were actually terrified when each plague was happening.

Q on the commentator
This *Rashi* is difficult to understand. Why were the Jewish People scared when the plagues occurred? Moshe warned them a few weeks before each plague. During the first one, the entire Nile turned to blood for the Egyptians but not for the Jews. When the second plague hit, frogs infested the Egyptians' clothing, food, and ovens, but they did not hop into any Jewish homes. Every plague afflicted only the Egyptians, not the Jews. Furthermore, the Jewish People understood that the cause behind the plagues was to break the Egyptians, while G-d showed his love for us. So why the fear?

New insight
We learn from this *Rashi* an amazing lesson. Although intellectually the Jews knew that there was nothing to fear, on an emotional level, they could not watch the destruction and devastation without feeling that perhaps they would be harmed as well. Experiencing such intense chaos all around them had a very real effect on their psyches.

Lesson for life
Fear can blind us from thinking straight. It can render ineffective even the intellectually gifted person. If the generation that saw miracles straight from G-d could feel this way, it certainly holds true for us. However, we must remember that there is so much we can accomplish if we can push back that fear. Just as an EMT, a doctor, or a nurse can override fear and rise to the occasion when dealing with a medical crisis, we too can conquer our fears. May we be blessed to put fear on hold and function with our intellect to help ourselves and assist others.

Growth through Torah

Dedicated by the Semmel family in memory
of their parents a"h
Yisroel Dovid and Alte Faiga Gittel Semmel
and Menachem Mendel and Breindel Kalish
Yosef Shmuel Lewkowicz

דברים לא:יב–יג: הַקְהֵל אֶת הָעָם הָאֲנָשִׁים וְהַנָּשִׁים וְהַטַּף וְגֵרְךָ
אֲשֶׁר בִּשְׁעָרֶיךָ לְמַעַן יִשְׁמְעוּ וּלְמַעַן יִלְמְדוּ וְיָרְאוּ אֶת ה' אֱלֹקֵיכֶם
וְשָׁמְרוּ לַעֲשׂוֹת אֶת כָּל דִּבְרֵי הַתּוֹרָה הַזֹּאת: וּבְנֵיהֶם אֲשֶׁר לֹא יָדְעוּ
יִשְׁמְעוּ וְלָמְדוּ לְיִרְאָה אֶת ה' אֱלֹקֵיכֶם כָּל הַיָּמִים אֲשֶׁר אַתֶּם חַיִּים
עַל הָאֲדָמָה אֲשֶׁר אַתֶּם עֹבְרִים אֶת הַיַּרְדֵּן שָׁמָּה לְרִשְׁתָּהּ:

ספורנו: ובניהם אשר לא ידעו שלא היו יודעים לשאול בהיותם
טף, ישמעו שמיעת האזן או ששמעו שנאמרו דברים בה, ולמדו
ישאלו בגדלם וילמדו מן המבינים.

P arashas *Vayelech* speaks about the beautiful mitzvah of
Hakhel, in which the entire nation assembles, and the
king reads the book of *Devarim* to all. This took place every
seven years during the Festival of Sukkos.

The Torah discusses the attendees:

> *Gather together the people—the men, the women, and the **small children**...so that they will hear and so that they will learn...and be careful to perform all the words of this Torah. **And their children who do not know**—they shall hear and they shall learn to fear Hashem, your G-d, all the days that you live on the land to which you are crossing the Jordan, to possess it. (Devarim 31:12–13)*

Q on the verse · *Sforno* is bothered by a question. Why include "**the small children...who do not know**" how to even ask a question? Why not leave them home with a babysitter?

A of the commentator · He answers that, although the small children do not know much, they will hear what is going on and ask others to explain *Hakhel* when they grow up. Therefore, you should not leave them home but rather should bring them with you.

Q on the commentator · This *Sforno* seems strange. It can be difficult to pack up these young children and, once there, to keep them quiet during the program. In addition, is it worthwhile for them to have this experience when they do not understand anything? Why not just put *Hakhel* into the curriculum of their Jewish studies or have the rabbi give a sermon about it each year, and they will only attend it once they are able to appreciate what is going on?

New insight · We learn from this *Sforno* an unbelievable lesson. While it is true that it is hard for parents to bring these small children, and they will not comprehend much, still it is so worthwhile. They will experience honoring the Torah on a grand scale. It is vital for them to get this exposure regardless of whether they learn about it in school or will also attend when they are older. We must not discount that they are gaining something necessary for their growth, even now. In addition, it will plant the seeds for a desire to explore the Torah as they grow older.

Lesson for life I have often heard people say that they no longer attend a Torah class because they could not fully comprehend the lesson. Sometimes it is because the speaker threw in some Yiddish or Hebrew, or at other times the class may have been just out of their grasp, beyond the level that they were on. This can be disheartening. We must know that many times, even if we do not fully understand what is being said, we are still gaining and should never discount that. This is how we grow. Let us be inspired by those who have stuck it out during tough times and have grown to be very knowledgeable. We too can do the same.

Sticks and Stones

*Dedicated by the Semmel family in memory
of their parents a"h
Yisroel Dovid and Alte Faiga Gittel Semmel
and Menachem Mendel and Breindel Kalish
Yosef Shmuel Lewkowicz*

דברים לא:יד: וַיֹּאמֶר ה' אֶל מֹשֶׁה הֵן קָרְבוּ יָמֶיךָ לָמוּת קְרָא אֶת יְהוֹשֻׁעַ וְהִתְיַצְּבוּ בְּאֹהֶל מוֹעֵד וַאֲצַוֶּנּוּ וַיֵּלֶךְ מֹשֶׁה וִיהוֹשֻׁעַ וַיִּתְיַצְּבוּ בְּאֹהֶל מוֹעֵד:

דברים רבה ט:ו: דָּבָר אַחֵר, הֵן קָרְבוּ יָמֶיךָ, לָמָּה נִגְזַר עָלָיו מִיתָה בְּזֶה הַלָּשׁוֹן הֵן, רַבָּנָן אָמְרֵי לָמָה הַדָּבָר דּוֹמֶה, לְאֶחָד שֶׁכִּבֵּד אֶת הַמֶּלֶךְ וְהֵבִיא לוֹ דּוֹרוֹן, חֶרֶב חַדָּה. אָמַר הַמֶּלֶךְ הַתִּיזוּ אֶת רֹאשׁוֹ בָּהּ. אָמַר לוֹ אוֹתוֹ הָאִישׁ, אֲדוֹנִי הַמֶּלֶךְ בַּמֶּה שֶׁכִּבַּדְתִּיךָ בָּהּ אַתָּ מַתִּיז אֶת רֹאשִׁי. כָּךְ אָמַר מֹשֶׁה, רִבּוֹנוֹ שֶׁל עוֹלָם בְּהֵן קִלַּסְתִּיךָ, שֶׁכֵּן כְּתִיב (דברים י, יד): הֵן לַה' אֱלֹקֶיךָ הַשָּׁמַיִם וּשְׁמֵי הַשָּׁמַיִם וגו', וּבְהֵן אַתָּה גּוֹזֵר עָלַי מִיתָה. אָמַר לוֹ הַקָּדוֹשׁ בָּרוּךְ הוּא שָׁכֵן רַע רוֹאֶה אֶת הַנְּכָנֳסוֹת וְאֵינוֹ רוֹאֶה אֶת הַיּוֹצְאוֹת, אָמַר לוֹ אִי אַתָּה זָכוּר בְּשָׁעָה שֶׁשְּׁלַחְתִּיךָ לִגְאֹל אוֹתָן מִמִּצְרַיִם וְאָמַרְתָּ לִי (שמות ה, א): הֵן לֹא יַאֲמִינוּ לִי, הֱוֵי הֵן קָרְבוּ יָמֶיךָ.

218

In *Parashas Vayelech*, Hashem tells Moshe, "**Hain** (Behold), your days are drawing near to die" (*Devarim* 31:14).

The commentator explains
The *Midrash Rabbah* tells us that Moshe complained to Hashem. He said it was inappropriate for G-d to have used the same word "*Hain*" to warn of his impending death **because Moshe had used that word previously to praise Him.** (Hashem did have an answer in response to Moshe's complaint, but if this were not the case, He would have agreed with him; see *Midrash Rabbah* for further details.)

The midrash continues with a parable: A man presents his king with an exotic sword as a gift. The king orders his men to use it to cut off the man's head. The man objects, "How can you utilize this very sword that I gave you as a gift to cut off my head? Even if I may be deserving of death in general, that is so wrong."

Q on the commentator
The midrash's parallel to the discussion between Moshe and Hashem does not make sense. Everyone in his right mind would agree with the commoner that the king's cruelty is beyond the pale. Moshe is *kvetching* that Hashem should not use a particular word to tell of his impending death—the same word that he used to praise Hashem. Why not? A word is not a tool of death like a sword. What is the big deal?

New insight
The midrash teaches us an amazing lesson. As horrible as it is to use a gifted sword to execute the giftee, it is equally painful to use Moshe's word as a tool to remind him of his impending death.

Lesson for life
Let us take the midrash's lesson to heart and realize how sensitive we should be with the words we use. Sometimes they are daggers that pierce the heart of the recipient. At other times, they can encourage people to strive for great heights, accomplishing dreams they never thought possible. Like a craftsman who hones his skills and tools to produce things of beauty, let us use our words to inspire and build up the people around us.

Proud versus Pride

Dedicated by the Liberman family in memory of
Hillel Liberman a"h
Hillel Dovid ben HaRav Nesanel Yosef tbldch"t

דברים לב:מד: וַיָּבֹא מֹשֶׁה וַיְדַבֵּר אֶת כָּל דִּבְרֵי הַשִּׁירָה הַזֹּאת
בְּאָזְנֵי הָעָם הוּא וְהוֹשֵׁעַ בִּן נוּן:

רבנו בחיי: הוא והושע בן נון. הזכירו הכתוב עתה בשם שהיה לו
מתחלה, שנאמר (במדבר יג) ויקרא משה להושע בן נון, ללמדך
שאעפ"כ שנתמנה במקום משה לא הגיס דעתו כלל אבל היה
משפיל עצמו כבתחלה, ולכן יקראנו הכתוב עתה באותו שם
עצמו שהיה נקרא בו בתחלה כדי להורות על מעלתו.

Parashas Haazinu talks about Moshe nearing his death as he passes the mantle of leadership to Yehoshua.

*Moshe came and spoke all the words of this song in the ears of the people, he and **Hoshea, son of Nun**. (Devarim 32:44)*

Q on the verse
Rabbeinu Bachaya is bothered by a question. Many years ago, Moshe changed Hoshea's name to Yehoshua by adding the Hebrew letter *yud*. Why does the verse here call him "**Hoshea, son of Nun**" once again, a name that had not been used since his youth?

A of the commentator
He answers that the verse is alluding to the fact that as Yehoshua was being appointed to take over from Moshe as leader of the Jewish People, he did not let it go to his head. Rather, he conducted himself in the same manner as he did during his youth when everyone called him Hoshea, son of Nun!

Q on the commentator
This Rabbeinu Bachaya is hard to comprehend. Why is the Torah praising Yehoshua for not having an ego here? He was the number one Torah scholar at that time (after Moshe) who immersed himself in G-d's Torah and worked tirelessly at perfecting his character traits. Would we think that excluded humility? Furthermore, many commentaries describe that just as the moon reflects the light of the sun, Yehoshua reflected the light of Torah and everything he learned from Moshe. Since Moshe was the humblest man to walk the planet, it stands to reason that Yehoshua was quite humble as well. Finally, it would be one thing to get a big head if his predecessor had died, but Moshe is still around, so how haughty could Yehoshua be?

New insight
We learn from this Rabbeinu Bachaya an important lesson in human psychology. Although Yehoshua worked on his humility and was refined in this area, his evil inclination could have convinced him even on the slightest level that he was now "hot stuff," and he could have easily become haughty even while his Rebbe was still alive and well. The Torah praises Yehoshua here for eliminating those natural feelings that could have seeped in.

Lesson for life
When we receive accolades or a promotion, it is a major challenge not to let it get to our heads. If Yehoshua had difficulty with this, we certainly do. Just as he conquered these feelings, we can as well. What do we do if we really have a tremendous talent to be proud of, or if we did a fantastic job? Shouldn't

we feel proud? The *mussar* books tell us that there is a way to appreciate our talents without it inflating our ego. We should realize that our G-d-given abilities increase our obligation to utilize these tools to better the world around us. If we focus on this responsibility, we will be productive and feel pride, but never full of ego or haughtiness. In this manner, we can truly fulfill our unique mission in the world.

The Power of Prayer

Dedicated by the Liberman family in memory of
Hillel Liberman a"h
Hillel Dovid ben HaRav Nesanel Yosef tbldch"t

דברים לב:מח-נ: וַיְדַבֵּר ה' אֶל מֹשֶׁה בְּעֶצֶם הַיּוֹם הַזֶּה לֵאמֹר: עֲלֵה אֶל הַר הָעֲבָרִים הַזֶּה הַר נְבוֹ אֲשֶׁר בְּאֶרֶץ מוֹאָב אֲשֶׁר עַל פְּנֵי יְרֵחוֹ וּרְאֵה אֶת אֶרֶץ כְּנַעַן אֲשֶׁר אֲנִי נֹתֵן לִבְנֵי יִשְׂרָאֵל לַאֲחֻזָּה: וּמֻת בָּהָר אֲשֶׁר אַתָּה עֹלֶה שָׁמָּה וְהֵאָסֵף אֶל עַמֶּיךָ כַּאֲשֶׁר מֵת אַהֲרֹן אָחִיךָ בְּהֹר הָהָר וַיֵּאָסֶף אֶל עַמָּיו:

רש"י: וידבר ה' אל משה בעצם היום הזה. בִּשְׁלוֹשָׁה מְקוֹמוֹת נֶאֱמַר בְּעֶצֶם הַיּוֹם הַזֶּה...לְפִי שֶׁהָיוּ יִשְׂרָאֵל אוֹמְרִים בְּכָךְ וְכָךְ אִם אָנוּ מַרְגִּישִׁין בּוֹ—אֵין אָנוּ מַנִּיחִין אוֹתוֹ, אָדָם שֶׁהוֹצִיאָנוּ מִמִּצְרַיִם וְקָרַע לָנוּ אֶת הַיָּם וְהוֹרִיד לָנוּ אֶת הַמָּן וְהֵגִיז לָנוּ אֶת הַשְּׂלָו וְהֶעֱלָה לָנוּ אֶת הַבְּאֵר וְנָתַן לָנוּ אֶת הַתּוֹרָה, אֵין אָנוּ מַנִּיחִין אוֹתוֹ, אָמַר הַקָּבָּ"ה הֲרֵינִי מַכְנִיסוֹ בַּחֲצִי הַיּוֹם וְכוּ' (ספרי)

באר בשדה: ומה שכתוב אם אנו מרגישים בו אין אנו מניחים אותו—אף על גב דאין אדם שליט ברוח הכונה שהיו ישראל מפישים ברחמים וקרא כתיב הן אל כביר לא ימאס והיו צועקים

223

ובוכים ושערי דמעה לא ננעלו אלא שהקדוש ברוך הוא השיב
חכמים אחור ודעתם סכל שלא נתנו אל לבם לעשות כן.

In *Parashas Haazinu*, Hashem warns Moshe of his impending death:

> *Hashem spoke to Moshe **on that very day**, saying:
> "Ascend to this mountain, and see the land of Canaan
> that I give to the Children of Israel as an inheritance,
> and die on the mountain where you will ascend, and be
> gathered to your people..." (Devarim 32:48–50)*

Q on the verse

Rashi is bothered by what the unique word choice of "**on that very day**" is coming to teach us.

A of the commentator

He answers that there are three times in the entire Torah when we use this language to describe people who were super motivated to carry out a plan, and "on that very day" Hashem shows them that they cannot carry out their plan. In this instance, we are discussing the strong will of the Jewish People to try to save Moshe from his impending demise.

Rashi (as expounded upon by the *Be'er Basade*) explains the Jewish People's plan. They meant to overturn the impending decree of death by organizing a mass prayer where they would have poured out their hearts and souls to change Hashem's mind. Hashem, however, derailed their plan from ever praying for Moshe "on that very day."

Q on the commentator

Rashi is mystifying. Moshe was on such a high spiritual level that he was considered equivalent to the entire Jewish People. On several occasions, his prayers saved the Jewish People from extermination. To overturn his own fate, he prayed 515 times to be allowed to enter the Land of Israel. How then did the Jewish People think that their prayers would be successful?

New insight

We learn from here just how well this generation understood the power of prayer. They knew that their pleas would reach Hashem Himself, had He only allowed it. They hoped on the last

day of Moshe's life that their prayers would storm the heavens
and go straight to Hashem, overturning the decree.

Let us tap into the powerful tool of prayer. Let us invest our
time, energy, and focus on connecting with Hashem, together
with the Jewish nation. Let us never underestimate what our
prayers can do for ourselves, our families, and for others.

V'ZOS HABERACHAH

The Value of Unity

*Dedicated by Dr. and Mrs. Jeffrey and Janis Savran
in memory of their parents Irving and Vivian Savran*

דברים לג:ה: וַיְהִי בִישֻׁרוּן מֶלֶךְ בְּהִתְאַסֵּף רָאשֵׁי עָם יַחַד שִׁבְטֵי
יִשְׂרָאֵל:

דעת זקנים: ויהי בישורון מלך בהתאסף וגו'. כלומר כשישראל
יחד באחוה ורעות אז הקדוש ברוך הוא מלך עליהם אבל בשעת
מחלוקת כביכול הם עושין כאלו אין הקב"ה מלך עליהם.

רא"ש: ויהי בישורון מלך. כלומר כשישראל יהיו ביחד באחוה
ובריעות אז הקב"ה מלך עליהם אבל בשעת המחלוקת כביכול
הם עושים כמי שאין הקב"ה מלך עליהם.

Parashas *V'zos Haberachah* describes Hashem's kingship
over the Jewish nation:

He became King *over Yeshurun when the numbers of
the nation gathered—**the tribes of Israel in unity**.
(Devarim 33:5)*

226

Q on the verse *Daas Zekeinim* and *Rosh* ask why the verse only highlights, "**He became King [when] the tribes of Israel are in unity.**" Isn't He *always* our king?

A of the commentator They answer, "When the Jewish People are getting along in unity, we have a oneness that is real and then Hashem is considered our King. However, when we have disputes among us, then *we're making it as if* Hashem is not our King, and G-d distances Himself as well."

Q on the commentator This *Daas Zekeinim* is difficult to understand. The apparent connection between our interpersonal relationships and Hashem's kingship is puzzling. "If I live a righteous life and have issues with a few people, how can it be that I do not consider Hashem as King? I have no problem with Hashem; my relationship with Him is great!"

New insight We learn from here an amazing lesson about what it takes to be a true *eved Hashem*. If one learns Torah, prays, and performs acts of kindness, yet does not get along with some people, there is something lacking. Hashem wants all his children to be in harmony. When we fight with others, it affects our relationship with Him and pushes Him away. That is why the verse says that Hashem is our King only when "the tribes of Israel are in unity."

Lesson for life One of the most important things to work on in our personal growth and service of Hashem is creating togetherness with those around us. It is easy to get along with our friends and those who share our interests and goals, but it takes much more effort to connect with those who are different from us and have a different outlook on life.

The Second Temple was destroyed because of baseless hatred amongst the Jewish People. The rabbis teach us that Hashem will bring the final redemption and build the everlasting Third Temple when we love one another and get along. May we do our part to make this a reality and merit to bring Mashiach speedily in our time.

Getting Your
Fair Share

*Dedicated by Dr. and Mrs. Jeffrey and Janis Savran
in memory of their parents Harry and Lillian Felberg*

דברים לד:א–ג: וַיַּעַל מֹשֶׁה מֵעַרְבֹת מוֹאָב אֶל הַר נְבוֹ רֹאשׁ
הַפִּסְגָּה אֲשֶׁר עַל פְּנֵי יְרֵחוֹ וַיַּרְאֵהוּ ה' אֶת כָּל הָאָרֶץ אֶת הַגִּלְעָד
עַד דָּן: וְאֵת כָּל נַפְתָּלִי וְאֶת אֶרֶץ אֶפְרַיִם וּמְנַשֶּׁה וְאֵת כָּל אֶרֶץ
יְהוּדָה עַד הַיָּם הָאַחֲרוֹן: וְאֶת הַנֶּגֶב וְאֶת הַכִּכָּר בִּקְעַת יְרֵחוֹ עִיר
הַתְּמָרִים עַד צֹעַר:

רלב"ג: ויעל משה מערבות מואב אל הר נבו וגו'. זכר שהראהו
השם יתעלה את כל הארץ את הגלעד עד דן. וידמה מזה שידע
משה בנבואה איזה חלק יגיע לכל השבטים ולזה אמר עד
דן...ואם תאמר אם ידע משה, למה לא הגביל העניין בתורה,
להגביל גורל כל אחד מהשבטים, כמו שהגביל כל הארץ. אמרנו
לך, שכבר רצה השם יתעלה שיהיה זה בגורל, להסיר התרעומת
והמחלוקת מישראל.

רלב"ג: התועלת התשיעי הוא להודיע שכבר נתפרסם ונודע
למשה בנבואה מה שהגיע מהארץ לשבט שבט וזה מבואר ממה

228

שנזכר מנחלת בנימין ובני יוסף וזבולון ויששכר ודן ונפתלי ואשר
ולזה יחויב שנודה שמה שהגיע על פי הגורל לשבט שבט הוא
היה הראוי לו לפי מה שגזר השם יתעלה ולזה יתבאר שמה' כל
משפט הגורל.

I n the final *parashah* of the Torah, Moshe says goodbye to the
Jewish People before passing away. G-d fulfills his promise to
let Moshe see the Land of Israel, although he does not enter it.

> *Moshe ascended from the plains of Moab to Mount
> Nebo, to the summit of the cliff that faces Jericho, and
> Hashem showed him the entire land: the Gilead as far
> as **Dan; all of Naphtali, and the land of Ephraim and
> Menasheh; the entire land of Yehudah** as far as the
> western sea…(Devarim 34:1–3)*

**Q on the
verse**

Ralbag (on this verse and *Toeles* 9) is bothered by a question.
When Moshe went up the mountain to look at the Land of
Israel, why does the verse tell us he saw each tribe's land? The
process of picking a *gorel* (lots) to decide which tribe received
what portion of land had not yet occurred. This only happened
once Yehoshua led them into battle against their enemies and
they entered the land. So how did Moshe see such a thing, and
if he did, why did he not share that information with the tribes?

**A of the
commentator**

He answers that Moshe knew from prophecy exactly which
lands would go to which tribes. That is why it says he saw the
"land of Dan, Naphtali, Ephraim, Menasheh, and Yehudah"!
The *Ralbag* explains, however, that Moshe was not supposed
to reveal this information at this time because a *gorel* would be
more conducive to avoid disputes regarding the fairness of the
land division. With a *gorel*, everyone would feel that his fate was
decreed by G-d, thereby avoiding any potential conflicts.

**Q on the
commentator**

This *Ralbag* is hard to understand. He is saying that had their
beloved Moshe come down from his mountain tour of the Holy
Land telling them the portions of land that they were to get

based on his prophecy, they would not trust him. There would be complaints and disputes. When they would make a *gorel*, however, they would trust it. Why?

New insight

We learn from this *Ralbag* an incredible lesson about the psyche of a person. Although the Jewish People knew intellectually that Moshe was sharing what G-d said about the land division, emotionally they would question the whole thing if they felt robbed of the estate to which they thought they were entitled. They would fight, complain, and ask for a recount. The *gorel* that would be done later by Yehoshua, however, would appear like a random activity, and they would trust that the results came straight from G-d.

Lesson for life

Very often, when it comes to dividing up assets, whether among business partners or family members, things can get sticky. This is not because people do not get along or do not trust one another, but because, when dealing with money, we all want to make sure that we get our fair share. By realizing that these situations are naturally more prone to result in arguments, we can be proactive in avoiding these issues before they arise. May we merit to always see the best in others and form lasting peaceful relationships.

Holidays

Rosh Hashanah

Dedicated Anonymously

בראשית כב:ד–ה: בַּיּוֹם הַשְּׁלִישִׁי וַיִּשָּׂא אַבְרָהָם אֶת עֵינָיו וַיַּרְא אֶת
הַמָּקוֹם מֵרָחֹק: וַיֹּאמֶר אַבְרָהָם אֶל נְעָרָיו שְׁבוּ לָכֶם פֹּה עִם הַחֲמוֹר
וַאֲנִי וְהַנַּעַר נֵלְכָה עַד כֹּה וְנִשְׁתַּחֲוֶה וְנָשׁוּבָה אֲלֵיכֶם:

רא״ש: שבו לכם פה עם החמור. מכאן ארז״ל עם הדומה לחמור
שנמשלים האומות לחמורים וא״ת תינח אליעזר שהוא כנעני
אבל ישמעאל למה נמשל לחמור והלא זרע קדש מצבתו זרע
אברהם קדוש ה' וי״ל דהכי קא' שאל להם אברהם כשנשא
את עיניו וראה את המקום אמר להם רואים אתם המקו' השיבו
שניהם לא ראינו מאומה אמר להם שבו לכם פה עם החמור כיון
שאין אתם רואים מקום שכינה שורה הרי אתם נחשבים כבהמה
שאינה רואה ואינה מרגשת בקדושה וזהו עם הדומה לחמור לענין
ראייה והשגחה ולא לענין הזרע שיהא מתדמה זרעם לזרע בהמה
שהרי אחד מיהא היה זרע קדש כדפירשנו.

In the Torah reading for Rosh Hashanah, Avraham instructs
his son Yishmael and servant Eliezer to stay behind while he
and his son, Yitzchak, go to bring an offering to Hashem.

233

*On the third day, Avraham raised his eyes and perceived the place from afar. And Avraham said to the young men, "**Stay here by yourselves with the donkey, while I and the lad will go yonder;** we will worship and we will return to you." (Bereishis 22:5)*

Q on the verse

The *Rosh* asks, "Why does the Torah record that Avraham told Yishmael and Eliezer, '**Stay here by yourselves with the donkey,** while I and Yitzchak go further'"? It is akin to saying, "Stay in the car, while we take care of business." But why record it for posterity?

A of the commentator

He answers with an important lesson. When they arrived at this place, it was engulfed in G-d's holiness. It would later become known as the holiest place on earth where both the First and Second Temple would be built. When asked if the young men sensed something extraordinary, they replied in the negative. Avraham then told them, "If you cannot feel the sanctity, you are compared to a donkey that cannot sense it." That is the meaning behind the words, "stay here by yourselves with the donkey."

Q on the commentator

This *Rosh* sounds harsh. Just because they do not sense the holiness, Avraham rebuked them. What did they do wrong? Not everyone feels such things. Some people are more sensitive than others.

New insight

This *Rosh* teaches us an amazing life lesson. If Avraham reprimanded them for not feeling the spirituality, that means it was within their grasp to be attuned to such a phenomenon. This is something they should have worked on, and yet they did not. Even though they were great in many areas, they fell short in this.

Lesson for life

I once had a Rosh Yeshiva who was formerly a congregational rabbi. He used to share the following story:

One of my congregants returned from his first tour of the Land of Israel and ran straight to my office sharing his incredible experiences with me. He spoke with excitement about how he toured here and there and thoroughly enjoyed it. "But," he concluded, "I think the Western Wall is overrated. I went to pray there, and I did not feel anything." The rabbi told him, "The problem isn't with the Wall. The problem is with you!"

We are not always "tuned in" to the channel of spirituality. However, it is something that we can be receptive to if we only make more of an effort. It is also a worthwhile endeavor to connect ourselves with the Creator who has given us so much.

During Rosh Hashanah time, we experience a closer connection to the Master of the Universe and have a heightened sensitivity to spirituality. We know that G-d draws near to us and that He is rooting for us to come closer to Him. May we have a happy, healthy, sweet new year filled with blessings and spirituality.

Yom Kippur

Dedicated Anonymously

וַיִּקְרָא טז:לב–לד: וְכִפֶּר הַכֹּהֵן אֲשֶׁר יִמְשַׁח אֹתוֹ וַאֲשֶׁר יְמַלֵּא אֶת
יָדוֹ לְכַהֵן תַּחַת אָבִיו וְלָבַשׁ אֶת בִּגְדֵי הַבָּד בִּגְדֵי הַקֹּדֶשׁ: וְכִפֶּר אֶת
מִקְדַּשׁ הַקֹּדֶשׁ וְאֶת אֹהֶל מוֹעֵד וְאֶת הַמִּזְבֵּחַ יְכַפֵּר וְעַל הַכֹּהֲנִים
וְעַל כָּל עַם הַקָּהָל יְכַפֵּר: וְהָיְתָה זֹּאת לָכֶם לְחֻקַּת עוֹלָם לְכַפֵּר
עַל בְּנֵי יִשְׂרָאֵל מִכָּל חַטֹּאתָם אַחַת בַּשָּׁנָה וַיַּעַשׂ כַּאֲשֶׁר צִוָּה ה'
אֶת מֹשֶׁה:

רש"י: ויעש כאשר צוה וגו'. כְּשֶׁהִגִּיעַ יוֹם הַכִּפּוּרִים עָשָׂה כַּסֵּדֶר הַזֶּה;
וּלְהַגִּיד שִׁבְחוֹ שֶׁל אַהֲרֹן, שֶׁלֹּא הָיָה לוֹבְשָׁן לִגְדֻלָּתוֹ אֶלָּא כִּמְקַיֵּם
גְּזֵרַת הַמֶּלֶךְ.

O n Yom Kippur, the holiest day of the year, the High
Priest would enter the Holy of Holies adorned with special clothing and offer the purest of prayers to achieve complete
forgiveness on behalf of the entire Jewish People.

*This shall be to you an eternal decree to bring atone-
ment upon the Children of Israel for all their sins once*

236

*a year; **and Aharon did as Hashem commanded Moshe**. (Vayikra 16:32–34)*

Q on the
verse
Rashi is bothered by a question. Why did the Torah need to point out that "**Aharon did as Hashem commanded Moshe**"? Was there any doubt he would do exactly as instructed?

A of the
commentator
He answers that not only did Aharon follow Hashem's directives to the tee, but he is being praised that when he put on the additional garments of the High Priest, he did it solely for the purpose of serving the King, meaning G-d.

Q on the
commentator
This *Rashi* is difficult to understand. As the emissary to plead with Hashem to forgive the nation from all sins, wipe the slate clean, and start fresh, Aharon had been entrusted with the most important job on Yom Kippur. He must stay up all night the evening before his service in the Tabernacle. He entered the Holy of Holies just this once over the course of the year and knew that if he did not keep his prayers on track for the entire time, not only wouldn't he satisfy his objective, but he would be punished severely. Do we really need to state that he kept his thoughts pure of ulterior motives while wearing the garments of the High Priest? Would he really think, "Wow, I look really nice in these new threads, don't I?"

New
insight
We learn from this *Rashi* an important life lesson. Of course, Aharon, as the High Priest, understood his vital mission at the time. He also appreciated the purpose of wearing the holy clothing for Heaven's sake and not for his own purposes. However, with all this, it is possible for even the greatest of men to be affected on a slight level and feel a little unkosher pride while walking around in such magnificent clothing. That is why the Torah praised him for staying 100 percent focused and not allowing ulterior motives to seep in, even one iota.

Lesson
for life
We know that in the Hebrew month of Elul, which proceeds Rosh Hashanah, Hashem comes closer to us, yearning for us to make a stronger spiritual connection with Him. During the Ten

Days of Repentance, He roots for us to utilize this time to do a little better than before, and He will, G-d-willing, write us in the Book of Good Life for the upcoming year, even if we are not totally deserving. He just wants to see us make an effort. Let us try our best to do more mitzvos during this time with total devotion, connecting to the King of the World, and let us be sealed in the Book of Life.

Sukkos

ויקרא כג:מא–מב: וְחַגֹּתֶם אֹתוֹ חַג לַה' שִׁבְעַת יָמִים בַּשָּׁנָה חֻקַּת
עוֹלָם לְדֹרֹתֵיכֶם בַּחֹדֶשׁ הַשְּׁבִיעִי תָּחֹגּוּ אֹתוֹ: בַּסֻּכֹּת תֵּשְׁבוּ שִׁבְעַת
יָמִים כָּל הָאֶזְרָח בְּיִשְׂרָאֵל יֵשְׁבוּ בַּסֻּכֹּת:

חזקוני: כל האזרח בישראל ישבו בסכת...חג זה נקבע בזמן
אסיפת גרן ויקב פן ירום לבבם על בתיהם שהם מלאים כל טוב
ויאמרו ידינו עשתה לנו את כל החיל הזה ומתוך שישבו בסוכה
יתנו שבח שבח והודיה למי שנתן להם נחלה ובתים מלאים כל טוב.

O n the holiday of Sukkos, we read the following verses:

*You shall dwell in booths for a seven-day period; **every
native in Israel shall dwell in booths**. So your generations will know that I caused the Children of Israel
to dwell in booths when I took them from the land of
Egypt...(Vayikra 23:41–42)*

239

Q on the verse The *Chizkuni* asks about the reasoning behind the commandment that "**every native in Israel shall dwell in booths.**"

A of the commentator He answers that all Jews have this special mitzvah at this time of year to leave the comforts of our palatial homes and sit in the sukkah because it is the time of the harvest. Right after we gather and fill our homes with our bountiful produce, we start to feel haughty. Therefore, G-d says, "I'm giving you this mitzvah to go out of your home and focus on Me."

Q on the commentator This *Chizkuni* is hard to digest. Perhaps some ego-inclined individuals will feel that way and need to see their rabbi or therapist, but surely this should not be a reason to institute this mitzvah for posterity for the entire Jewish nation.

New insight We learn from this *Chizkuni* an amazing truth in human psychology! He is teaching that naturally, when a person brings in all his home-grown produce, it is inevitable that he will have feelings of pride that go straight to his head. He will think, "Look how great a businessman I am. I used the correct product to protect the crops from infestation and I watered them just right." When he is counting his money, it is all about him. Some people experience this reaction in the extreme; others feel it to a lesser degree. An element of ego due to one's success is present for all on some level, no matter how slight, and even in the greatest of men.

Lesson for life Let us use this Sukkos holiday season to dwell in our huts under the stars and connect simply with G-d. He protected us from the elements in the desert and surrounded us with the holy Clouds of Glory on all sides, just like our sukkah. Let us relive this miracle every Sukkos and cherish Him and all that He does for us. Let us share this invaluable lesson with our entire family.

Chanukah

Dedicated by Ally and Alex Levin
in honor of their parents

במדבר ז:יב: וַיְהִי הַמַּקְרִיב בַּיּוֹם הָרִאשׁוֹן אֶת קָרְבָּנוֹ נַחְשׁוֹן בֶּן
עַמִּינָדָב לְמַטֵּה יְהוּדָה:

חזקוני: נחשון בן עמינדב לא נקרא כאן נשיא כדי שלא יתגאה
על שהקריב ראשון וכל האחרים נקראו נשיאים לפי שהשפילו
עצמם והקריבו אחריו.

The Torah reading for Chanukah is found in *Parashas Naso* and speaks about the Tabernacle dedication. There were twelve leaders of the tribes who each independently came up with the idea of bringing an offering at the dedication to Hashem. Hashem honors them here for posterity by not only recognizing each one separately for his contribution, but accords them six verses each to describe their offerings, even though all those offerings were identical.

*The one who brought his offering on the first day
was Nachshon, son of Amminadav, of the tribe of
Yehudah…(Devarim 7:12)*

Q on the verse   The *Chizkuni* is bothered by a question. Why does the Torah call each person by the name *nasi* (leader) except for the first one? Here it only says, "**the one who brought his offering.**" He was also a *nasi*, yet the Torah leaves out his title. Why?

A of the commentator   He answers that had the verse said, "Nachshon the Leader brought his offering first," it would have caused him to feel haughty. Therefore, the Torah leaves out that word to remind him to be humble.

Q on the commentator   This *Chizkuni* is astounding. Nachshon and all the leaders were great men who worked on character refinement, including humility. We also know from several commentaries that Nachshon deserved to go first either from his own merits or from those of his tribe, so if the Torah called him the *nasi*, what difference should it make?

New insight   We learn from this *Chizkuni* an amazing lesson about the innate human desire for recognition. Even though Nachshon was eager to do a mitzvah and had no intention of looking for honor, once the Torah listed him, it was hard to not enjoy the spotlight. Although there were good reasons for listing him first, he could still feel a slight sense of ego. Therefore, Hashem "erased" the word *nasi* from his title in order to help him stay focused.

Lesson for life   The old joke goes that someone steps up on stage when being honored and says "Oh, shucks, I never wanted to be honored and really all the people here in the audience are the real heroes here tonight. I don't need any of this *kavod*." Meanwhile, he is muttering under his breath to his dear friend, "Do they know who I am? Why isn't the plaque larger?"

We all have those moments in life when we get involved in a mitzvah with no intention of receiving honor in return. Once people begin to honor us, however, or we see others being commended for their good deeds, it is so easy to get caught up in such things. May we always do things solely for the right reasons, and may we be blessed immeasurably for those pure mitzvos that we do.

Purim

*Dedicated by Rabbi Moshe and Mrs. Pessel Goldstein
in memory of Yehuda Leib ben Bentzion Halevi*

אסתר ז:ה: וַיֹּאמֶר הַמֶּלֶךְ אֲחַשְׁוֵרוֹשׁ וַיֹּאמֶר לְאֶסְתֵּר הַמַּלְכָּה מִי הוּא זֶה וְאֵי זֶה הוּא אֲשֶׁר מְלָאוֹ לִבּוֹ לַעֲשׂוֹת כֵּן:

רש״י: וַיֹּאמֶר הַמֶּלֶךְ אֲחַשְׁוֵרוֹשׁ וַיֹּאמֶר לְאֶסְתֵּר הַמַּלְכָּה. כָּל מָקוֹם שֶׁנֶּאֱמַר: "וַיֹּאמֶר, וַיֹּאמֶר" שְׁנֵי פְעָמִים, אֵינוֹ אֶלָּא לְמִדְרָשׁ, וּמִדְרָשׁוֹ שֶׁל זֶה: בַּתְּחִלָּה הָיָה מְדַבֵּר עִמָּהּ עַל יְדֵי שָׁלִיחַ. עַכְשָׁיו שֶׁיָּדַע שֶׁמִּמִּשְׁפַּחַת מְלָכִים הִיא, דִּבֶּר עִמָּהּ הוּא בְּעַצְמוֹ.

The Book of Esther tells how Haman hated the Jews and got permission from King Achashverosh to set a national holiday to wipe out the Jewish People. The great sage Mordechai, uncle of Queen Esther, advises his niece not to share her nationality with King Achashverosh until absolutely necessary.

When Esther reveals her identity to the king as a Jewess, the decree is annulled, and the Jews are saved.

244

> **And he said**—*King Achashverosh,* **and he said** *to Esther the Queen, "who is the person who wants to harm you and your people?" (Esther 7:5)*

Q on the verse   *Rashi* is bothered by a question. Why is the phrase **"and he said"** written twice in the verse?

A of the commentator   He answers that it is alluding to two different speakings. First, the king spoke to Esther through a messenger; then, after learning that she descended from Jewish royalty, he started to speak directly to her. (Don't ask me how this marriage ever made it this far, for this implies that he never spoke directly to his wife until now.)

Q on the commentator   What does *Rashi* mean? Just because he found out her lineage, he viewed her in a totally different light and treated her with more respect? She was the same person, wife, and queen as she was just five minutes ago. Nothing changed, so why did he shift his whole demeanor toward her?

New insight   We learn from this *Rashi* the following lesson. When King Achashverosh thought that Esther really was undeserving of the throne but for her marriage to him, he treated her as such. He only spoke to her through a messenger and looked down upon her as a lowly commoner. He was unable to break free from that perception. However, upon learning about her royal lineage, he was able to open his eyes and realize her true value.

Lesson for life   We often judge others based on their appearances and actions. We perceive a person with a certain backdrop of what we think is real. If tomorrow we found out, however, that a person comes from royalty or is a billionaire, we should not change how we treat that person, but the reality is that we would! We should always value people for who they are by recognizing their true virtues. In that way, we will not be fooled by what society is telling us should be important, and we will truly value them.

Pesach

*Dedicated by Alexandra Cender in honor of her son
Zachai Binjamin (Zachary Gordon) Cender*

שמות יד:כא–כג: וַיֵּט מֹשֶׁה אֶת יָדוֹ עַל הַיָּם וַיּוֹלֶךְ ה' אֶת הַיָּם
בְּרוּחַ קָדִים עַזָּה כָּל הַלַּיְלָה וַיָּשֶׂם אֶת הַיָּם לֶחָרָבָה וַיִּבָּקְעוּ הַמָּיִם:
וַיָּבֹאוּ בְנֵי יִשְׂרָאֵל בְּתוֹךְ הַיָּם בַּיַּבָּשָׁה וְהַמַּיִם לָהֶם חֹמָה מִימִינָם
וּמִשְּׂמֹאלָם: וַיִּרְדְּפוּ מִצְרַיִם וַיָּבֹאוּ אַחֲרֵיהֶם כֹּל סוּס פַּרְעֹה רִכְבּוֹ
וּפָרָשָׁיו אֶל תּוֹךְ הַיָּם:

רמב״ן: ויט משה את ידו על הים ויולך ה' את הים ברוח קדים וגו'
היה הרצון לפניו יתברך לבקע הים ברוח קדים מיבשת שיראה
כאלו הרוח היא המחרבת ים, כענין שכתוב (הושע יג טו) יבא
קדים רוח ה' ויבוש מקורו וחרב מעיינו, השגיא למצרים ויאבדם,
כי בעבור זה חשבו אולי הרוח שמה הים לחרבה, ולא יד ה'
עשתה זאת בעבור ישראל, אע״פ שאין הרוח בוקעת הים לגזרים
לא שמו לבם גם לזאת, ובאו אחריהם מרוב תאותם להרע להם,
וזה טעם וחזקתי את לב פרעה ורדף אחריהם, שחזק לבם לאמר
ארדוף אויבי ואשיגם בים, ואין מידי מציל, ולא זכרו עתה כי ה'
נלחם להם במצרים.

T he seventh day of Pesach commemorates the anniversary of the splitting of the sea.

> *Moshe stretched out his hand over the sea, and Hashem moved the sea with a strong east wind all night, and He turned the sea to damp land and the water split. The Children of Israel came within the sea on dry land; and the water was a wall for them, on their right and on their left. Egypt pursued and came after them...into the midst of the sea. (Shemos 12:21–23)*

Q on the verse *Ramban* asks: Were the Egyptians crazy? Even the biggest, windiest hurricanes do not split the sea in half with walls on each side producing dry land at their feet. Didn't they clearly see the hand of G-d? And if so, why risk their lives?

A of the commentator He answers that even though the Egyptians should have seen clearly, they did not. Had they stopped to think for an instant, they would not have continued. Due to their burning desire to harm the Jews, they did not take this scene to heart. *Ramban* continues that besides ignoring this supernatural feat, they also blocked out all that had happened to them during the ten plagues. Those events should have shaken them to their core, yet they did not. That is why they signed their death warrants and marched into the sea, only to have it come crashing down upon them.

Q on the commentator This *Ramban* seems wild. There are people eager to harm others, but would not jump off a cliff to accomplish that. Also, we know that the superpower Egypt had gone from a thriving country to ruins in the last year, thanks to G-d. They were reeling from the plague of the firstborns, which had recently transpired, and the Torah teaches that all the plagues did not hold a candle to the phenomenon of the splitting of the sea. So, it is still hard to understand why they followed the Jewish People into the Red Sea.

New insight *Ramban* teaches us that the Egyptians had a tremendous desire driving them and were no longer thinking logically. They first blocked out their experiences of the last ten months of plagues and then ignored the supernatural phenomenon happening before their eyes. This desire to harm the Jewish People caused them to see the world through warped lenses, which ultimately resulted in their deaths.

Lesson for life We often find ourselves in similar yet less extreme scenarios. Sometimes, we are so focused on doing something negative that we ignore all the indications that it is improper. At other times, we are trying to accomplish great things and ignore issues that should stop us. During this Pesach season, let us focus our attention on accomplishing vital things while being aware of real issues that arise.

Shavuos

*Dedicated by Michele Berman in memory
of her parents Ruth and Lewis Fialkoff*

רלב"ג: התועלת העשירי. הוא להודיע שהוא ראוי לגמול חסד
למי שיגמלהו לו או לקרוביו. הלא תראה כי מפני החסד שעשתה
רות לנעמי שהיתה אשת קרובו התעורר לעשות לרות זה החסד
שנזכר בזאת המגלה עד שכבר הפליג בזה ורצה להטיב לה
באופן שלא תרגיש בו כדי שלא תתבייש מזה והוא מה שצוה
שישולו לה מן הצבתים וכבר עשה לה כל זה בעבור החסד
שעשתה לנעמי כמו שספר מצורף אל זה מה שהראתה מטוב
לבבה עם ה' יתברך בבואה לחסות תחת כנפיו ולזאת הסבה
תמצא מפני החסד שעשתה רות לנעמי והיתה עושה לה תמיד
התעוררה נעמי לבקש לה מנוח אשר ייטב לה ונתנה לה עצה
נתיישרה בה להנשא לבועז.

רש"י רות א:ז: וַתֵּצֵא מִן הַמָּקוֹם. לָמָּה נֶאֱמַר? הֲרֵי כְּבָר נֶאֱמַר:
"וַתֵּשֶׁב מִשְּׂדֵי מוֹאָב", וּמֵהֵיכָן תָּשׁוּב אִם לֹא תֵצֵא מִן הַמָּקוֹם
שֶׁהָיְתָה שָׁם? אֶלָּא מַגִּיד שֶׁיְּצִיאַת צַדִּיק מִן הַמָּקוֹם נִכֶּרֶת וְעוֹשָׂה
רֹשֶׁם. פָּנָה זִיוָהּ, פָּנָה הֲדָרָהּ, פָּנָה שִׁבְחָהּ שֶׁל עִיר. וְכֵן "וַיֵּצֵא יַעֲקֹב
מִבְּאֵר שָׁבַע".

249

רש"י רות א:יט: וַתֵּלַכְנָה שְׁתֵּיהֶם. אָמַר רַבִּי אַבָּהוּ, "בֹּא וּרְאֵה
כַּמָּה חֲבִיבִים הַגֵּרִים לִפְנֵי הַקָּדוֹשׁ בָּרוּךְ הוּא. כֵּיוָן שֶׁנָּתְנָה דַעְתָּהּ
לְהִתְגַּיֵּיר, הִשְׁוָה אוֹתָהּ הַכָּתוּב לְנָעֳמִי."

The Book of Rus, read on Shavuos, tells the story of a Moabite princess named Rus who was dedicated to becoming Jewish and following the Torah. She persevered to join her mother-in-law Naomi on a journey from Moav to Israel after the passing of their husbands, leaving her non-Jewish family behind. She was committed to remaining by her mother-in-law's side, selflessly devoted to her welfare.

The commentator explains
The *Ralbag* (*Toeles* 10) tells us that Rus's *chessed* (kindness) and self-sacrifice towards Naomi subsequently motivated Naomi to match up the widowed Rus with the greatest rabbi of the generation, Boaz. As a result of the marriage, Rus became the progenitor of Jewish royalty: King David and King Shlomo come from this line, and ultimately so will Mashiach.

Q on the commentator
The *Ralbag* infers that had Naomi not deeply appreciated her daughter-in-law's kindness, she would never have thought of the match. This is puzzling, as *Rashi* (1:7,19) tells us that Naomi was extremely pious, and it stands to reason that she was someone who was always looking to do for others.

New insight
We learn from the *Ralbag* a key insight: One who is naturally motivated to do for others can be further motivated to reach even higher levels of generosity by recalling the kindness previously done for him.

Lesson for life
Let us take a moment to emulate Naomi during this Shavuos and reflect on the people in our lives—those around us have made us who we are today. We now can reciprocate. This is more than just "paying it forward." It is calling up a friend to whom you have not spoken in months, giving a smile, grocery shopping for a neighbor, etc. Let us be inspired to perform greater levels of *chessed*, especially to those who have helped us in so many ways.

Biographies
of Commentators

The biographies below are of Rishonim and Acharonim referenced herein. They are based on the Bar-Ilan University Responsa Project, *Shem Hagedolim* by Rav Chaim Yosef David Azulai (the *"Chida"*), *Shemos Chachamim* by Rav Avraham Weiss, and other sources. Compiled by Rabbi Chaim Goldstein.

Chizkuni—Rabbi Chizkia ben Manoach Chizkuni (thirteenth-century France) authored a commentary on the Pentateuch that incorporates and expands upon interpretations of *Rashi*, the *Ibn Ezra*, the *Rashbam* and other earlier commentators. According to his preface, Rav Chizkia chose to omit the names of the commentators he quotes (other than *Rashi*), so that readers would not evaluate a comment based upon the source's reputation but rather on its own merits: "Do not look at the barrel but at the wine poured from it." *Chizkuni* is regarded as one of the first "super-commentaries" on *Rashi's* commentaries. Little is known about his life, but he is quoted by the *Ramban*, *Minchas Yehudah*, *Maharsha*, and *Maharal* of Prague.

Daas Zekeinim—A compilation of commentaries on the Pentateuch authored by the *Baalei Ha'tosafos*, a group of Talmudic scholars predominantly from France, Germany, and England who followed a specific methodology of Talmudic analysis. The earliest *Baalei Ha'tosafos* were students of *Rashi* who lived in the twelfth century (such as the *Rashbam*), and the latest lived in the late thirteenth century or early fourteenth century (such as the *Rosh* and the *Minchas Yehudah*). The identity of the compiler of their commentaries is unknown.

Gur Aryeh—A super-commentary on *Rashi's* commentary on the Pentateuch authored by Rabbi Yehudah Loeve ben Bezalel, better known as the *Maharal* of Prague (c. 1520–1609). The *Maharal* served as the leading rabbi of Prague (now in the Czech Republic) and of Pozna, Poland. He was also the Rosh Yeshiva of a yeshiva he founded in Prague. He had several famous disciples, including Rabbi Yom Tov Lipman Heller (author of the *Tosafos Yom Tov*) and Rabbi David Ganz (author of the *Tzemach David*). The *Maharal* authored books on a very wide range of topics, including *Netzach Yisrael* (on Mashiach and redemption), *Gevuras Hashem* (on the Exodus from Egypt), *Derech Hachaim* (on Tractate *Avos*), and *Chiddushei Aggados* (on the parables and esoteric teachings of the Talmud). Many legends are tied to his name; the most famous is the story of the Golem of Prague, in which the Jewish community of Prague was saved from a severe blood libel.

Maharzu—Acronym for Moreinu HaRav Zev Wolf Einhorn of Vilna (died in 1862), who authored the *Peirush HaMaharzu*, a comprehensive commentary on the *Midrash Rabbah*. The *Maharzu* also authored a commentary on *Pirkei D'Rabbi Eliezer* (an early midrash), entitled *Midrash Tannaim*, and a commentary on *Pesikta Rabasi*, another midrash.

Midrash Rabbah—The most famous volumes of the midrash, a genre of Rabbinical literature that contains selections from the halachic and/or aggadic teachings of the Tanna'im and Amora'im arranged according to the verses of the Torah. Midrashim often bring many stories and parables to glean lessons and insights on the Torah.

Mizrachi—A super-commentary on *Rashi's* commentary on the Pentateuch authored by Rabbi Eliyahu Mizrachi (c. 1450–1526) of Constantinople. The *Mizrachi* addresses questions on *Rashi* raised by commentators such as the *Ramban* and the *Ibn Ezra*, and often elucidates why *Rashi* chose his explanation of a Biblical passage over other, alternative explanations. Rav Eliyahu served as Chief Rabbi of the Ottoman Empire. He was a well-respected halachic authority as well as a tireless community leader who cared for the poor, and he assisted the Jewish immigrants who were exiled from Spain in 1492. He was also a gifted mathematician who supplemented his income in his younger years teaching mathematics and logic.

Nachlas Yaakov—A super-commentary on *Rashi's* commentary on the Pentateuch, authored by Rabbi Yaakov Salnik (late sixteenth / early seventeenth century). The *Nachlas Yaakov* frequently critiques the *Mizrachi's* comments on *Rashi* and often offers an alternative approach.

Rabbeinu Bachya—Rabbeinu Bachya ben Asher (c. 1255–1340) was a student of the *Rashba* in Barcelona, Spain. His commentary on the Pentateuch is somewhat based upon the commentary of the *Ramban*, who was his teacher's teacher, and contains a mixture of simple explanation of the text, midrashim, philosophical analysis, and mysticism. Rabbeinu Bachya also authored *Kad Hakemach*, a treatise on ethics, prayer, and faith; *Sova Semachos*, a commentary on Job; and *Shulchan Shel Arba*, a halachic work. Rabbeinu Bachya should not be confused with the much earlier Rabbeinu Bachya ben Yosef ibn Pakuda, author of *Chovos Halevavos*.

Ralbag—Acronym for Rabbi Levi ben Gershon (1288–1344) of Provence, France. His maternal grandfather was the *Ramban*. A prodigious author, he wrote commentaries on Tanach and Mishnah, the philosophical work *Milchemes Hashem*, as well as secular treatises on astronomy, science, mathematics, and medicine. His commentary on the Bible is structured uniquely: Every section begins with a discussion of the literal meaning of the text followed by relevant ethical, philosophical, or halachic conclusions. He also invented an astronomical instrument that was used to measure the distance between stars or planets. A large crater on the moon, Rabbi Levi, was named in his honor.

Ramban—Acronym for Rabbi Moshe ben Nachman (1194–1270) of Gerona, Spain. He is regarded as one of the leading Torah sages of the Middle Ages and was leader of Spanish Jewry for several decades. Like *Rambam* and many other Spanish Rabbinic scholars, *Ramban* was a practicing physician. He wrote commentaries on the Pentateuch and the Talmud, several works on Jewish Law, and essays on mysticism and Jewish ethics. In 1263, the *Ramban* was forced by the Spanish king and clergy to debate a Jewish apostate and successfully defended Judaism, but the debate resulted in the *Ramban's* expulsion from Spain a few years later. At the age of seventy-three, the *Ramban* moved to Eretz Yisrael, where he reinvigorated the Jewish community in Jerusalem and taught Torah to numerous students in Acco.

Rashi—Acronym for Rabbi Shlomo Yitzchaki (1040–1105), the foremost commentator on the Torah as well as the Talmud. Born in Troyes, France, he traveled to Mainz and Worms to learn under Rabbi Yaakov ben Yakar and other students of Rabbeinu Gershom. *Rashi's* commentaries are considered a staple in understanding the Torah to this day and are quoted and analyzed by thousands of subsequent commentators. He came from an illustrious family that traced its ancestry back to King David. Out of humility, he never accepted a Rabbinic position and made his living as a wine merchant. His grandsons, the *Rashbam* and Rabbeinu Tam, were the first generation of Tosafists.

Rosh—Acronym for Rabbi Asher ben Yechiel (c. 1250–c. 1327). He lived in Germany for most of his life but fled to Spain in 1303 to escape corrupt noblemen who were attempting to hold him for ransom. He was a student of the Maharam M'Rottenberg, who was in turn a student of the *Baalei Ha'tosafos*, the authors of the *Tosafos* commentaries on the Talmud. Rav Asher authored a monumental halachic work organized in the order of the Talmud, which quotes extensively from the *Rif*, the leading Sephardic halachic authority prior to the *Rambam*, and also incorporates the analysis of the Ashkenazic *Baalei Ha'tosafos*. This work is one of the three compendiums of Jewish law that were primarily relied upon by Rabbi Yosef Karo in formulating his rulings in his *Shulchan Aruch*. In addition to the *Rosh's* halachic work, he wrote a *Tosafos* commentary on the Talmud, an ethical work called *Orchos Chaim*, and a commentary on the Pentateuch. His son, Rabbi Yaakov Baal Haturim, is the author of the *Tur Shulchan Aruch* and the *Tur* commentary on Pentateuch.

Sifsei Chachamim—A collection of super-commentaries on *Rashi's* commentary on the Pentateuch compiled by Rabbi Shabsai Bass (1641–1718) who lived in the Netherlands, Austria, Poland, and Germany. Rav Shabsai was a publisher and seller of Jewish books, as well as a noted bibliographer. Rav Shabsai was persecuted by the Jesuits and local authorities for publishing "blasphemous" material, and his books were sometimes confiscated. Nevertheless, he persevered in making Jewish scholarly works more accessible throughout Europe.

Sforno—Rabbi Ovadia Sforno (1470–1550) lived in Rome and Bologna, Italy. His commentary on the Pentateuch has become a favorite among scholars and laymen due to its clearness and simplicity. The commentary explains the Biblical text based upon its plain meaning and then derives lessons relating to human behavior and Jewish ethics. Rav Ovadia also wrote commentaries on *Shir Hashirim*, *Tehillim*, and *Koheles*. He did not wish to use his great knowledge of the Torah as a means of earning a livelihood, for the Torah was not given for profit. Instead, like the *Rambam* and others, he earned his livelihood as a physician.

Yalkut Shimoni—A comprehensive midrashic anthology covering the entire Tanach attributed to Rabbi Shimon HaDarshan of Frankfurt (thirteenth century). Sources quoted by the *Yalkut Shimoni* include the *Talmud Bavli*, the *Talmud Yerushalmi*, *Midrash Rabbah*, *Sifra*, *Mechilta*, and *Midrash Tanchuma*.

Index of Hebrew Names

Shemos: Exodus

Yaakov: Jacob

Yehoshua: Joshua

Yehudah: Judah

Yishmael: Ismael

Yisro: Jethro

Yitzchak: Isaac

Yocheved: Jochebed

Yosef: Joseph

About the Author

After completing a double rabbinic ordination from the Rabbinical Seminary of America (Chofetz Chaim) in Queens, Rabbi Shimon Feder founded the outreach organization Jewish Education Center of South Florida (JEC) in 2005 to combat rampant assimilation and apathy among South Florida Jews. The Boca Raton–based organization offers seven divisions for all ages: The Billi Marcus Camp Nageela Boca, Fun Family Hebrew School, Ohr Fellowships High School Program (with five divisions spanning from Boca Raton to Miami), FAU College Campus Outreach Program, Shabbat and High Holiday Program, Women's Programming, and Adult Programming. The JEC reaches approximately 525 people on a weekly basis.

Rabbi Shimon and Nechama Feder live in Boca Raton, Florida, with their six children, Moshe, Riva, Malka, Avraham, Adina, and Rusi.